CONTENTS

BUTTERFLY KISSES

Words and Music by RANDY THOMAS
and BOB CARLISLE

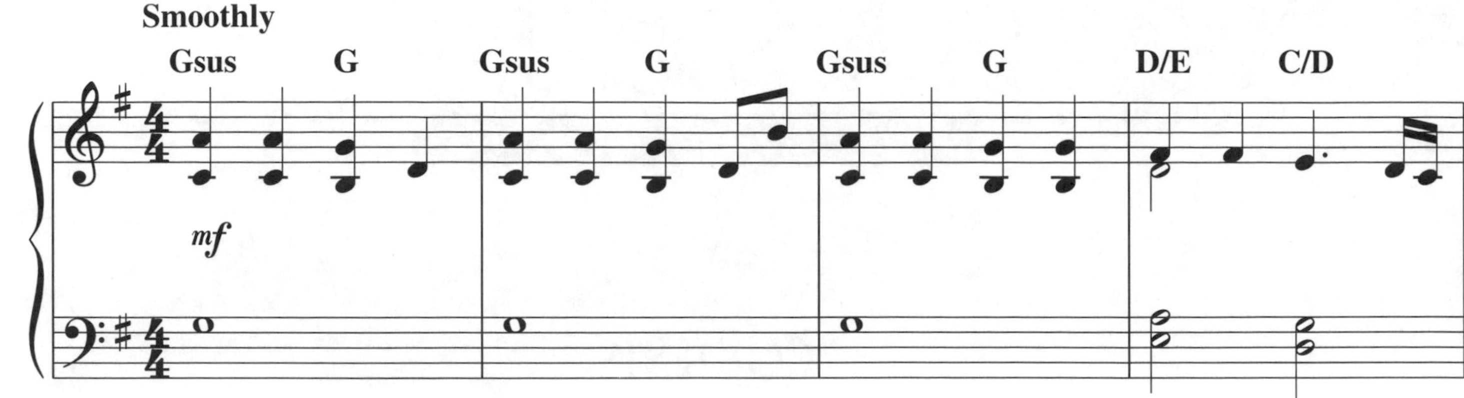

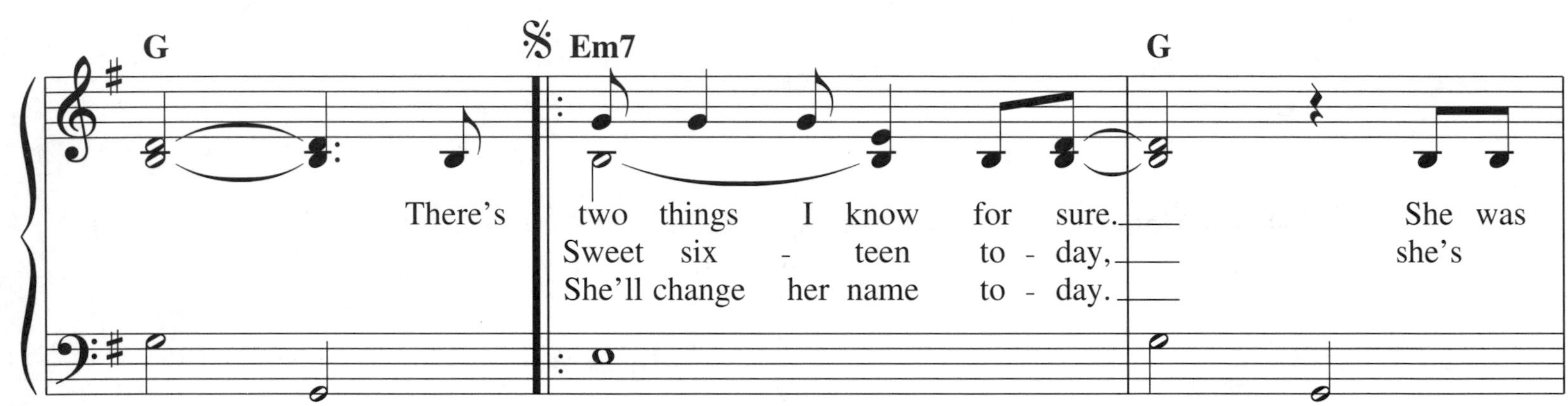

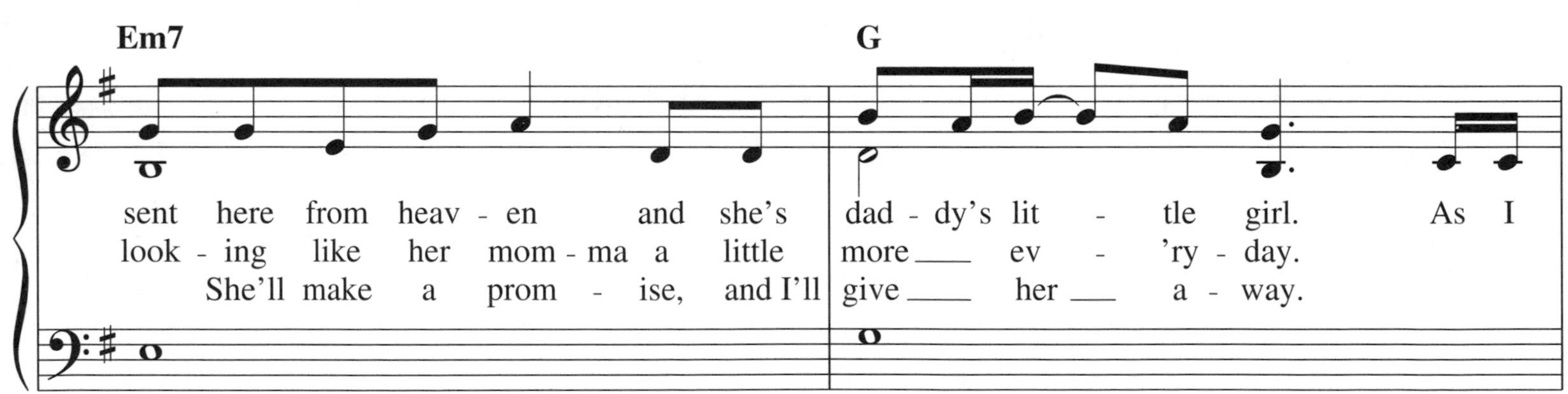

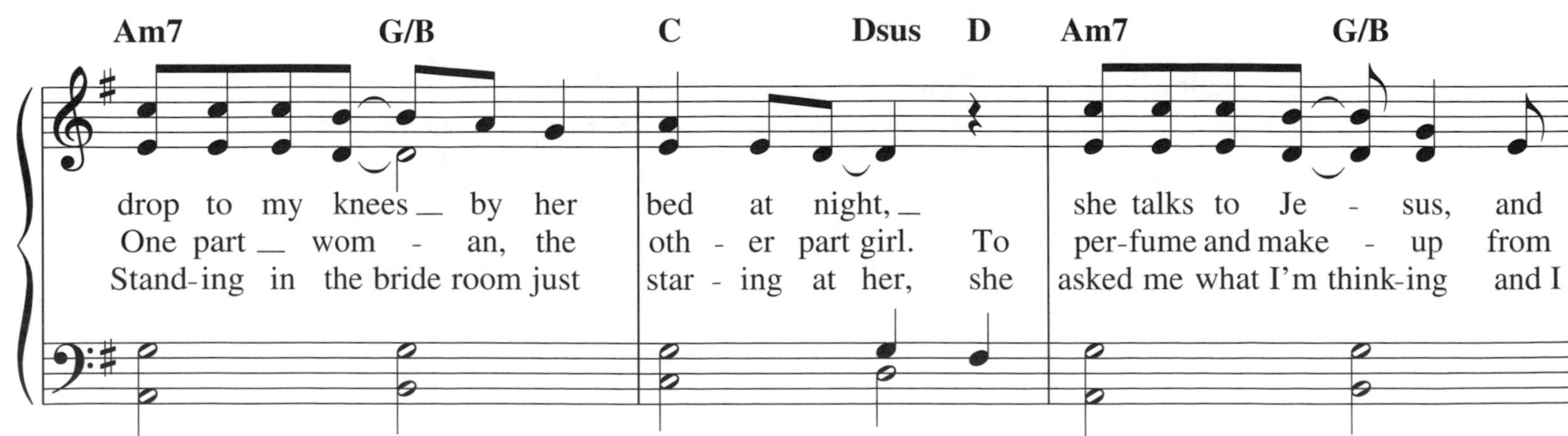

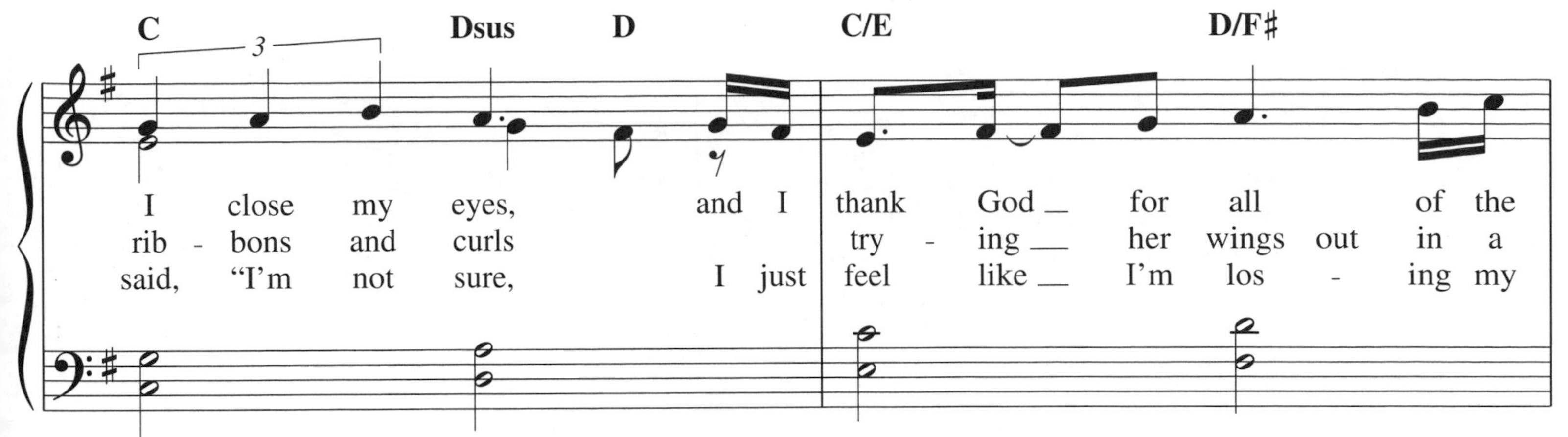
C Dsus D C/E D/F♯
3
I close my eyes, and I thank God for all of the
rib - bons and curls try - ing her wings out in a
said, "I'm not sure, I just feel like I'm los - ing my

G C D7sus
joy in my life. Oh, but most of all, for
great big world. But I re - mem - ber
ba - by girl." Then she leaned o - ver, gave me

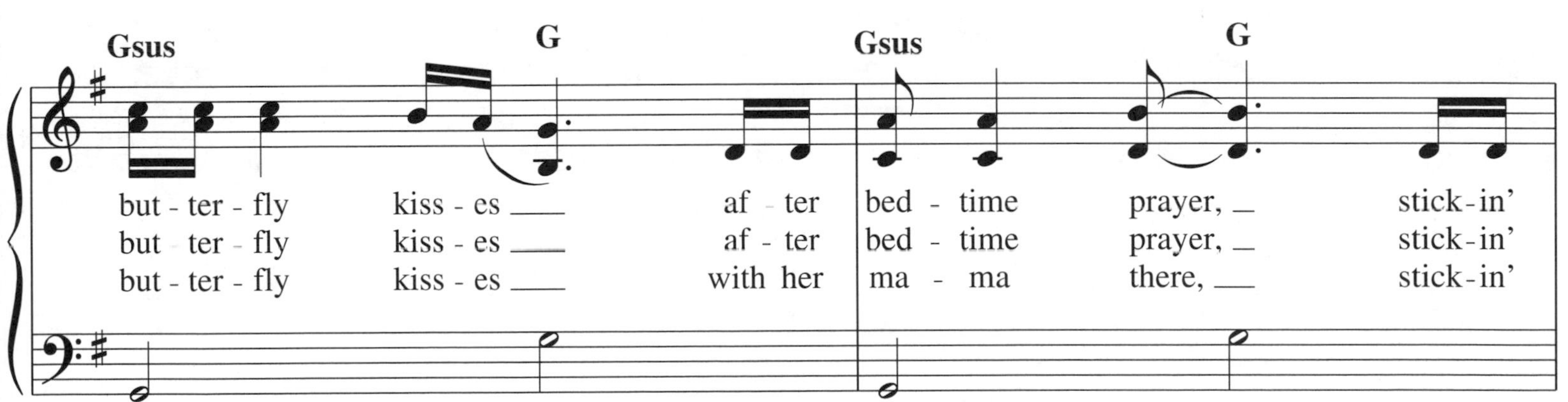
Gsus G Gsus G
but - ter - fly kiss - es af - ter bed - time prayer, stick-in'
but - ter - fly kiss - es af - ter bed - time prayer, stick-in'
but - ter - fly kiss - es with her ma - ma there, stick-in'

Gsus G Gsus Em D
lit - tle white flow - ers all up in her hair.
lit - tle white flow - ers all up in her hair. "You
lit - tle white flow - ers all up in her hair.

C
G/B
"Walk be - side the po - ny, dad-dy, it's my first ride. I
know how much I love you, dad-dy, but if you don't mind, I'm
Walk me down the aisle, dad-dy, it's just a - bout time. Does my

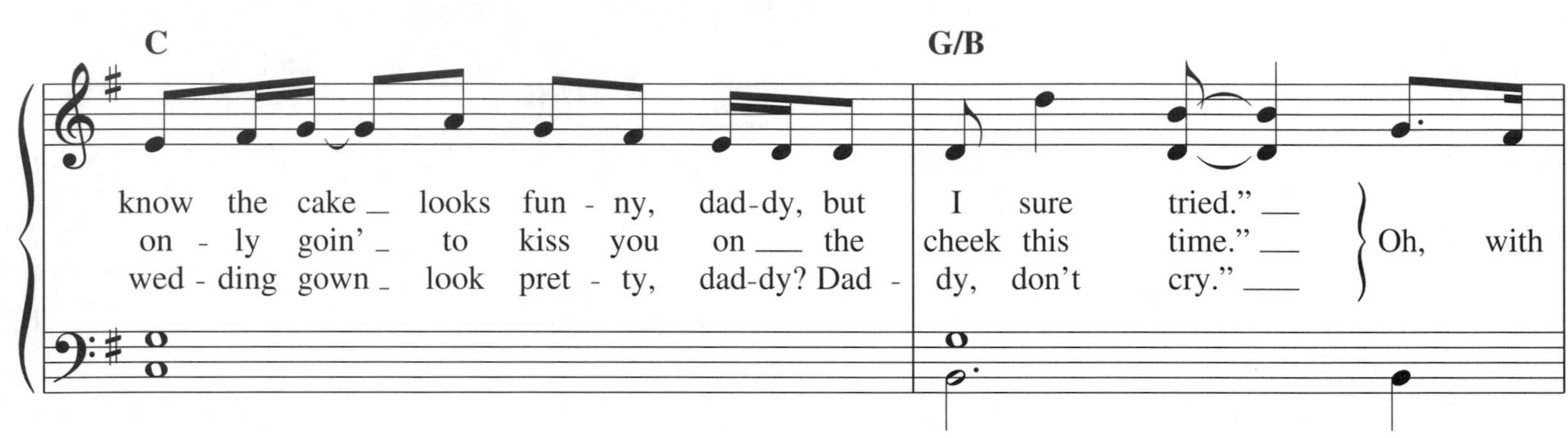
C
G/B
know the cake looks fun - ny, dad-dy, but I sure tried."
on - ly goin' to kiss you on the cheek this time."
wed - ding gown look pret - ty, dad-dy? Dad - dy, don't cry."
Oh, with

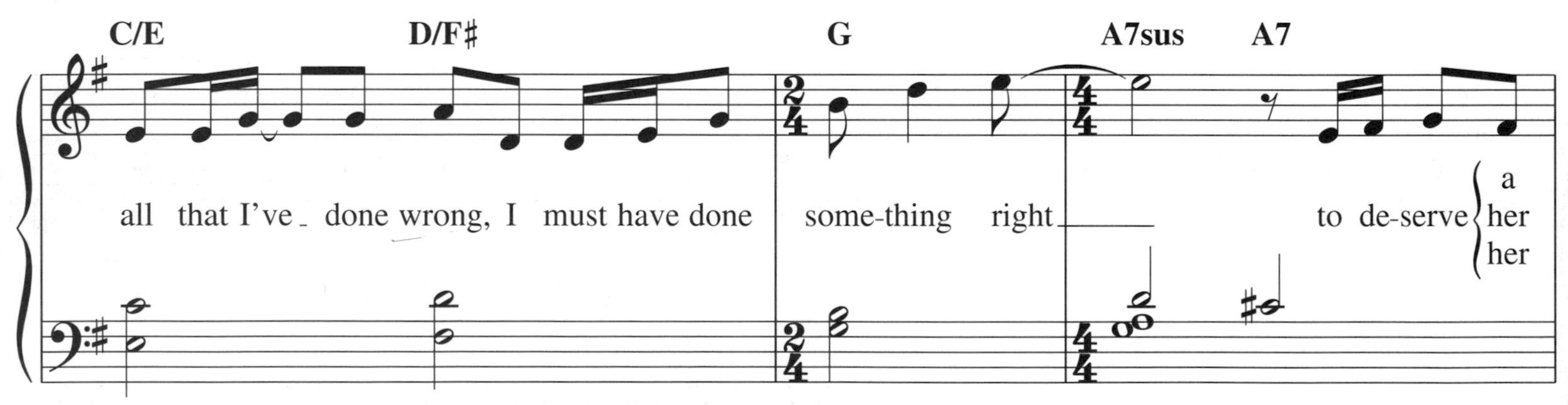
C/E
D/F#
G
A7sus
A7
all that I've done wrong, I must have done some-thing right to de-serve
a
her
her

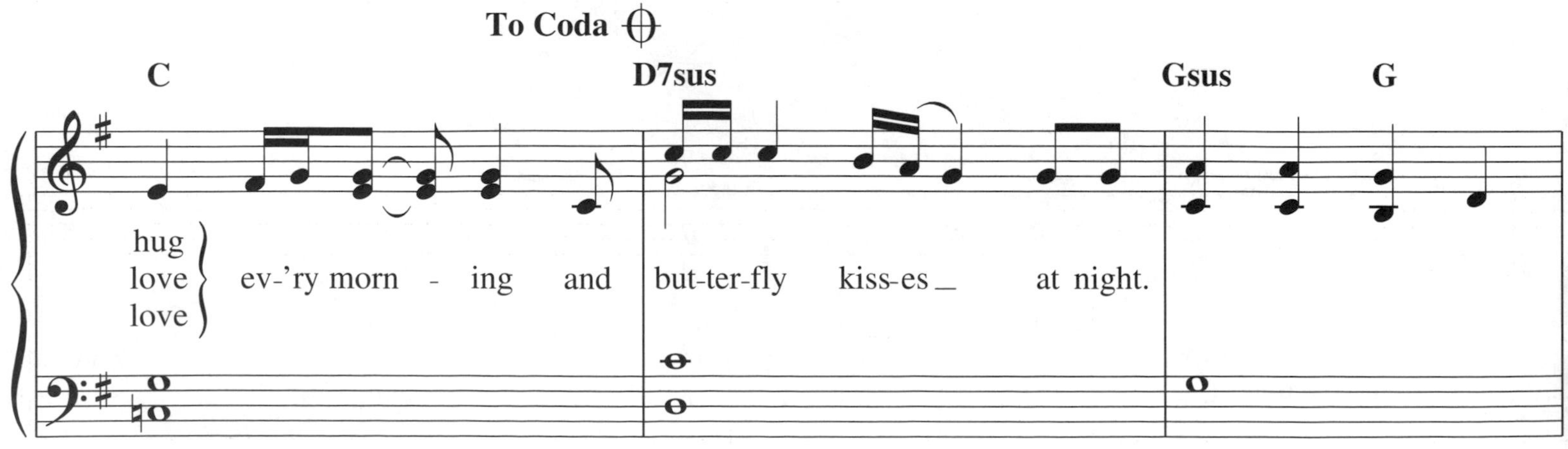
To Coda
C
D7sus
Gsus
G
hug
love
love
ev-'ry morn - ing and but-ter-fly kiss-es at night.

1.
Gsus
G
Gsus
G
D/E
C/D
G
2.
Gsus
G
B♭
D7sus/A
(All the pre-cious time.)
Like the
Gsus
G
Gsus
G
B♭
wind, the years go
by. (Pre-cious but-ter-fly,
D7sus/A
C/E
Am7
D7
D.S. al Coda
spread your wings and fly.)

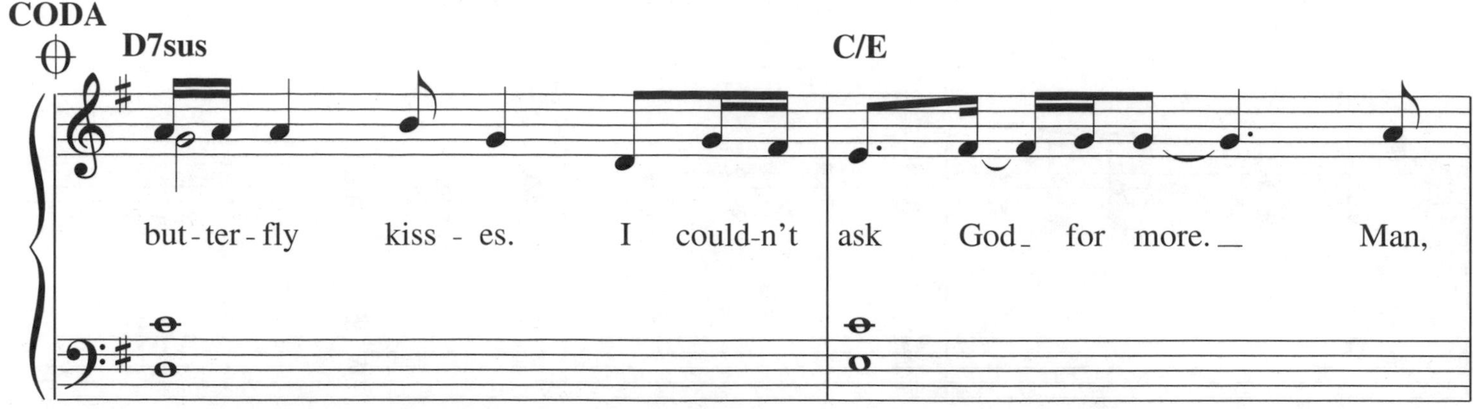
CODA
D7sus
C/E
but - ter - fly kiss - es. I could-n't
ask God for more. Man,

D/F♯
E♭maj7
G/D
this is what love is. I
know I've got to let her go, but I'll
al - ways re-mem-ber ev'ry
molto rit.
a tempo

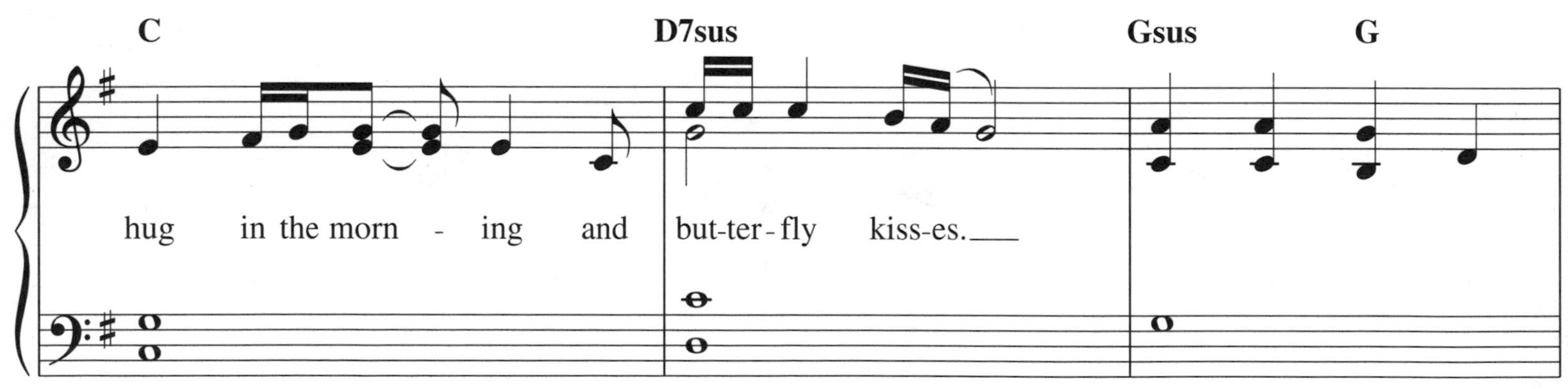
C
D7sus
Gsus
G
hug in the morn - ing and
but-ter - fly kiss-es.

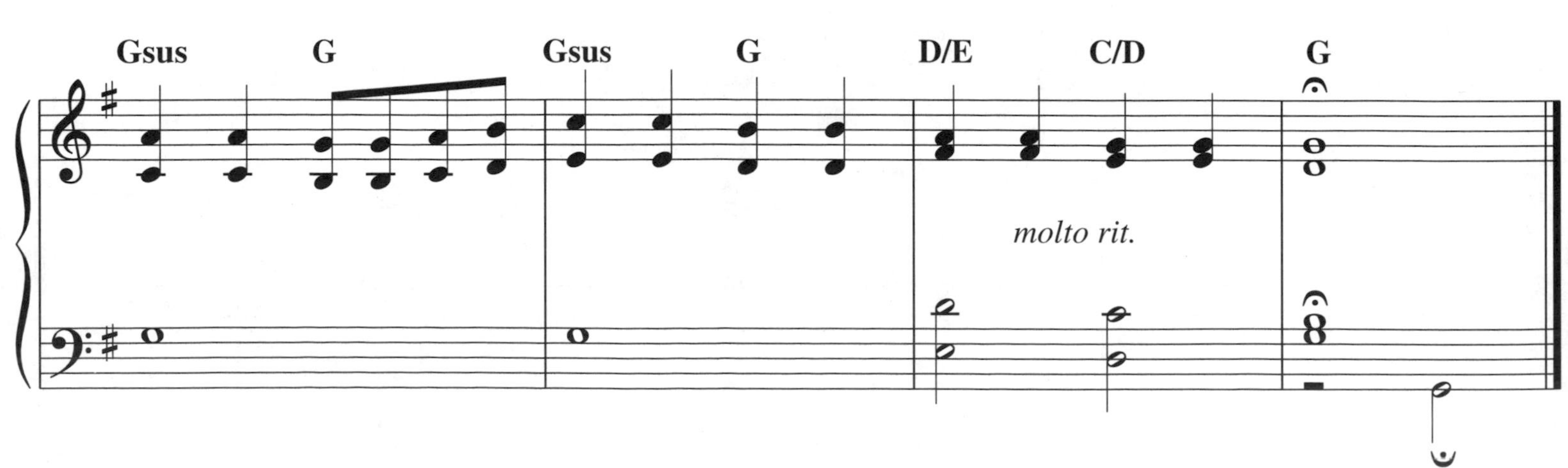
Gsus
G
Gsus
G
D/E
C/D
G
molto rit.

DON'T SPEAK

Words and Music by ERIC STEFANI
and GWEN STEFANI

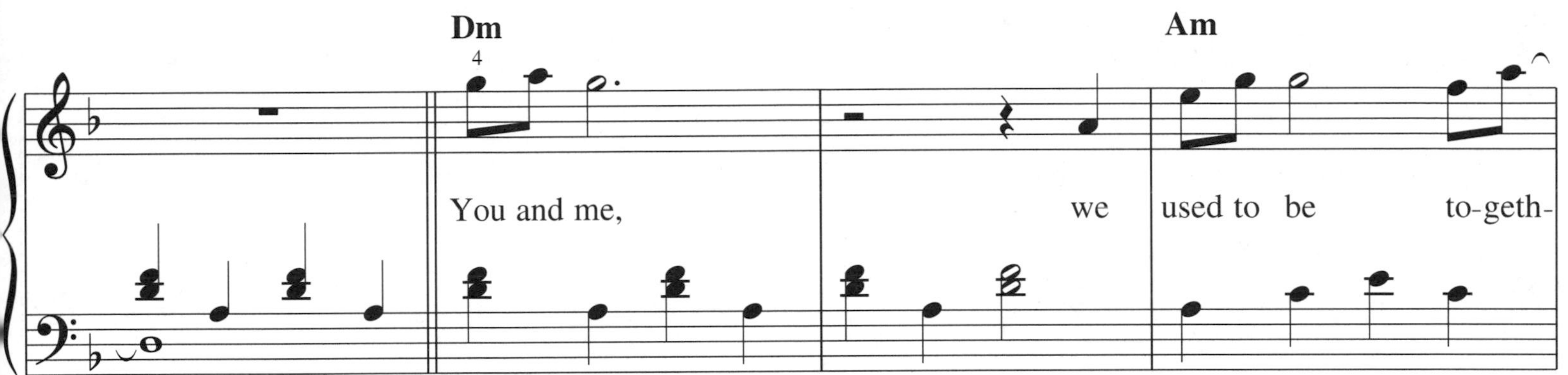

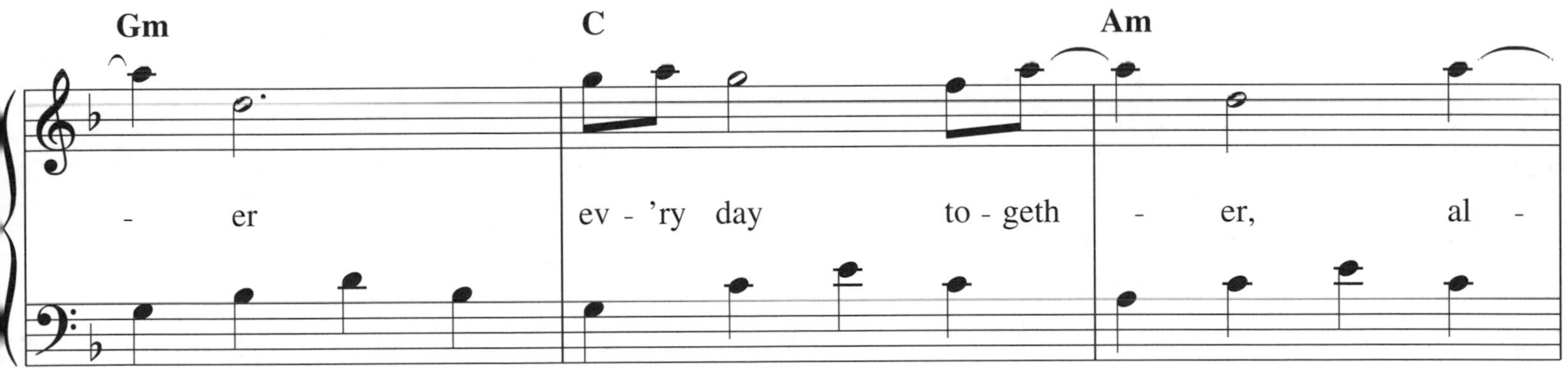

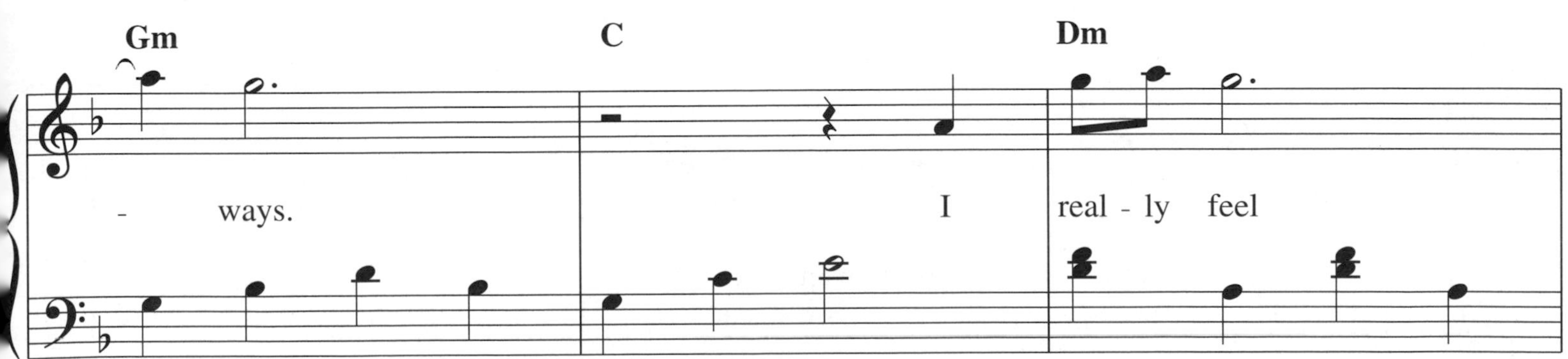

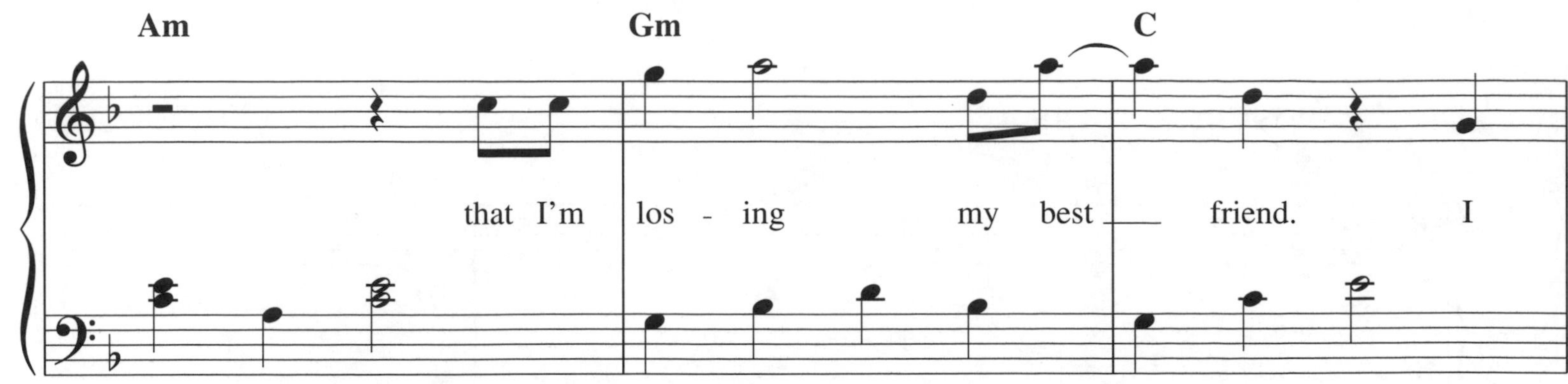
Am
Gm
C
that I'm los - ing my best friend. I

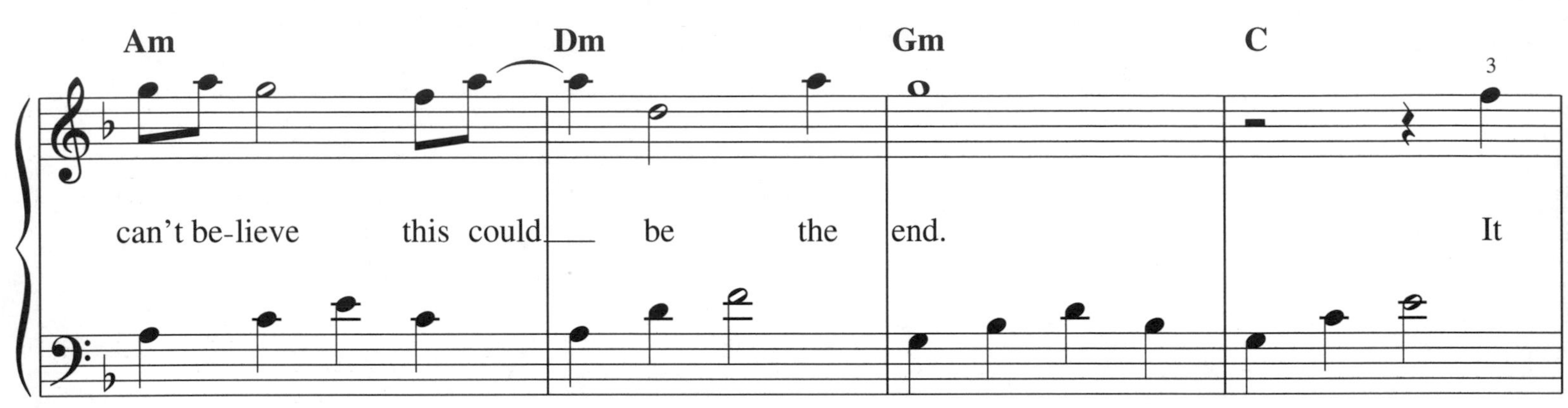
Am
Dm
Gm
C
3
can't be-lieve this could be the end. It

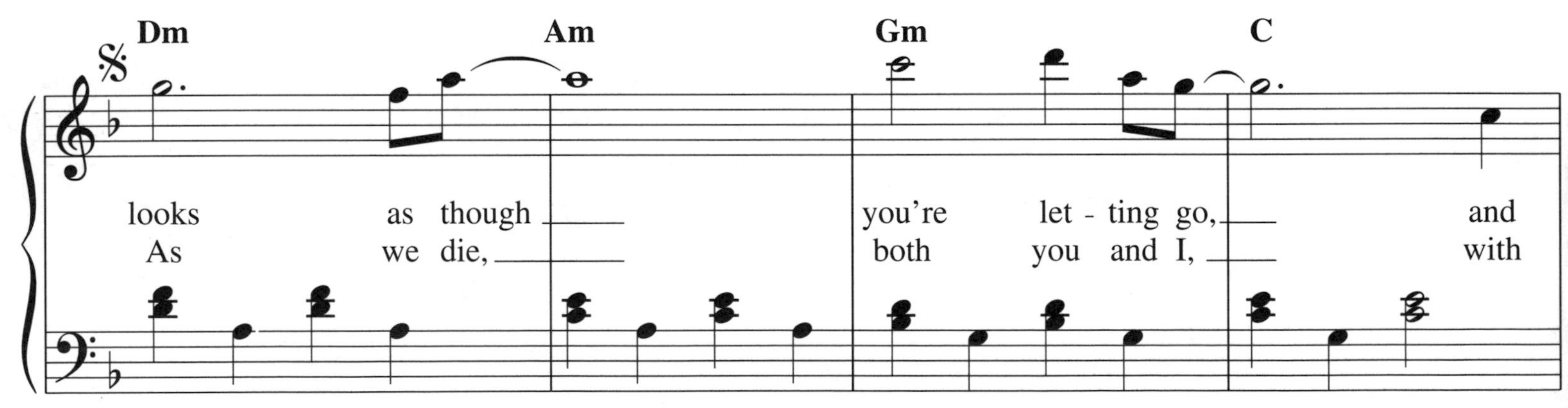
Dm
Am
Gm
C
looks as though you're let - ting go, and
As we die, both you and I, with

F
C
D
if it's real, well, I don't want to know.
my head in my hands I sit and cry.

Gm
Cm
F
Don't speak, I know just what you're say - ing,

D7
Cm
D7
Gm
so please stop ex-plain - ing. Don't tell me 'cause it hurts.

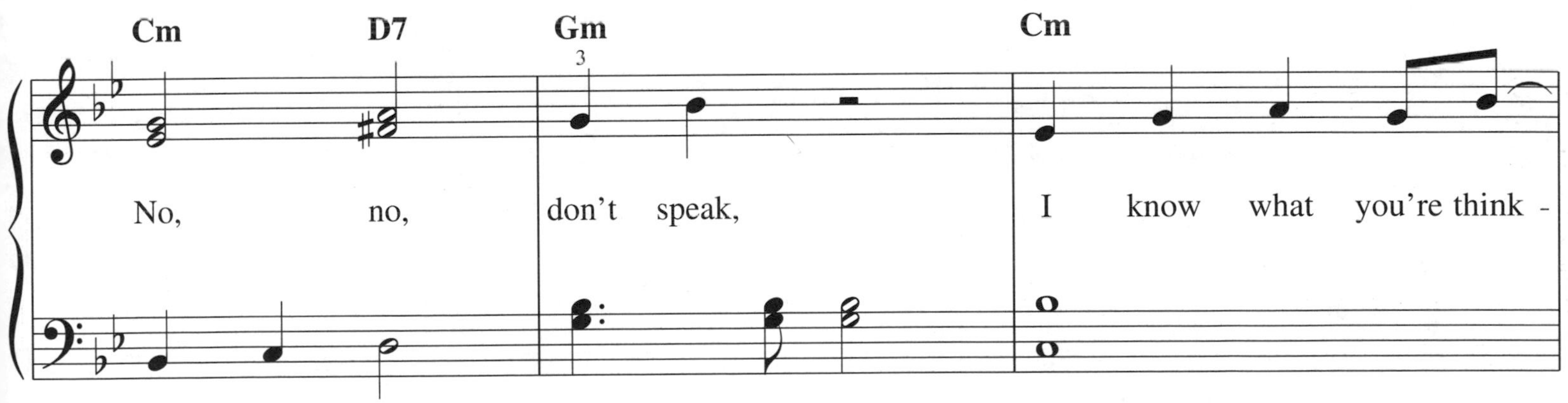
Cm
D7
Gm
Cm
No, no, don't speak, I know what you're think -

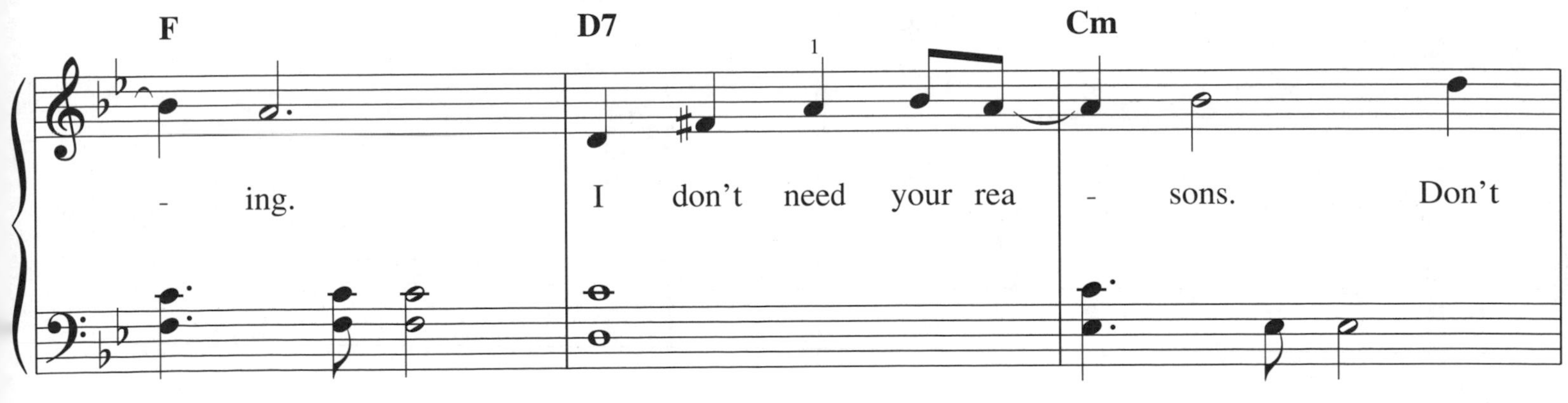
F
D7
Cm
- ing. I don't need your rea - sons. Don't

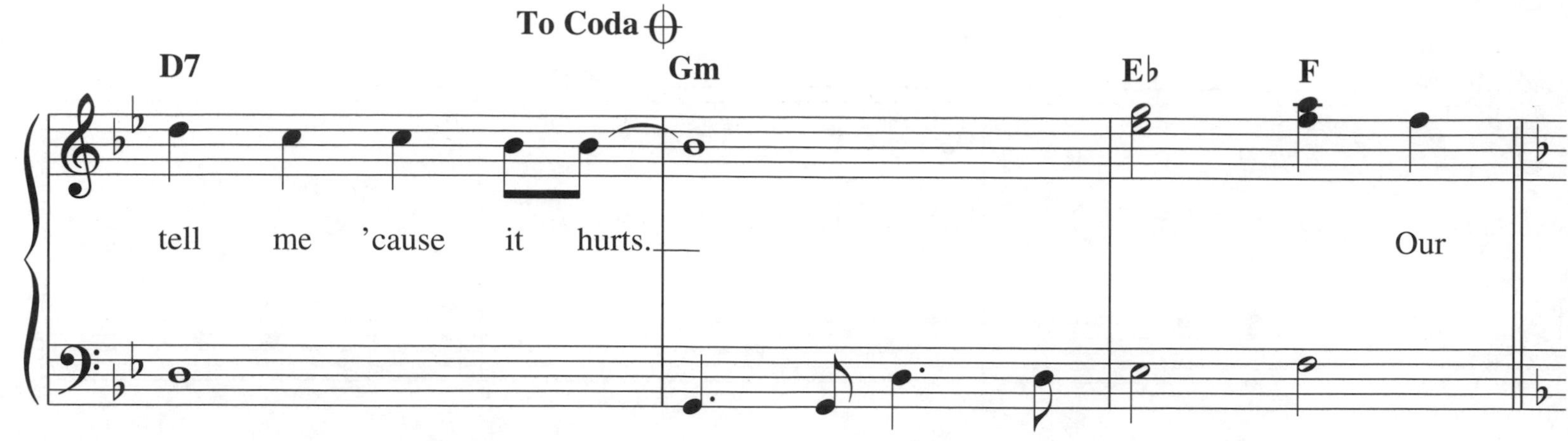
To Coda
D7
Gm
E♭
F
tell me 'cause it hurts.
Our

Dm
Am
mem - or - ies,
they can be in - vit -

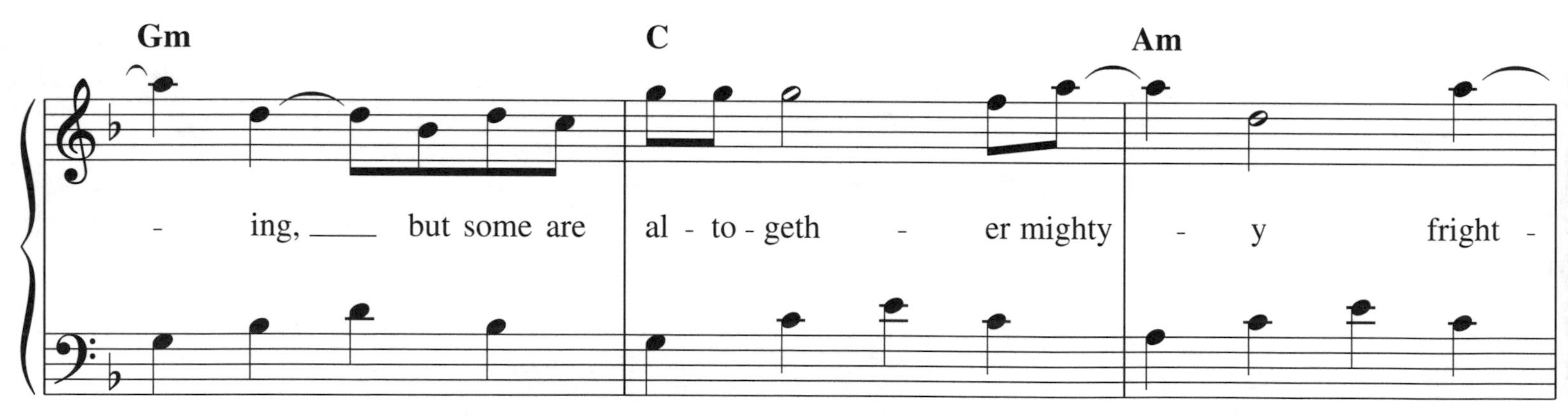
Gm
C
Am
- ing, but some are al - to - geth - er mighty - y fright -

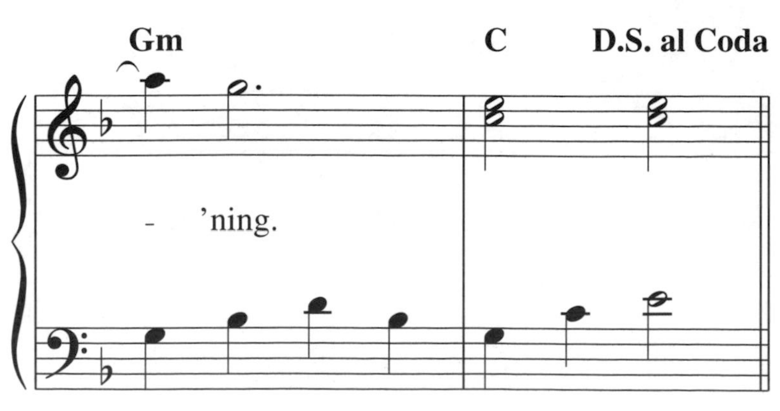
Gm
C
D.S. al Coda
- 'ning.

CODA
Gm

E♭
B♭/D
D♭
It's all end - ing, I got - ta stop pre - tend -

A♭/C
C♭
C♭(♭5)
- ing who we are.

B♭
Dm
Am

Gm
C
Am
Dm

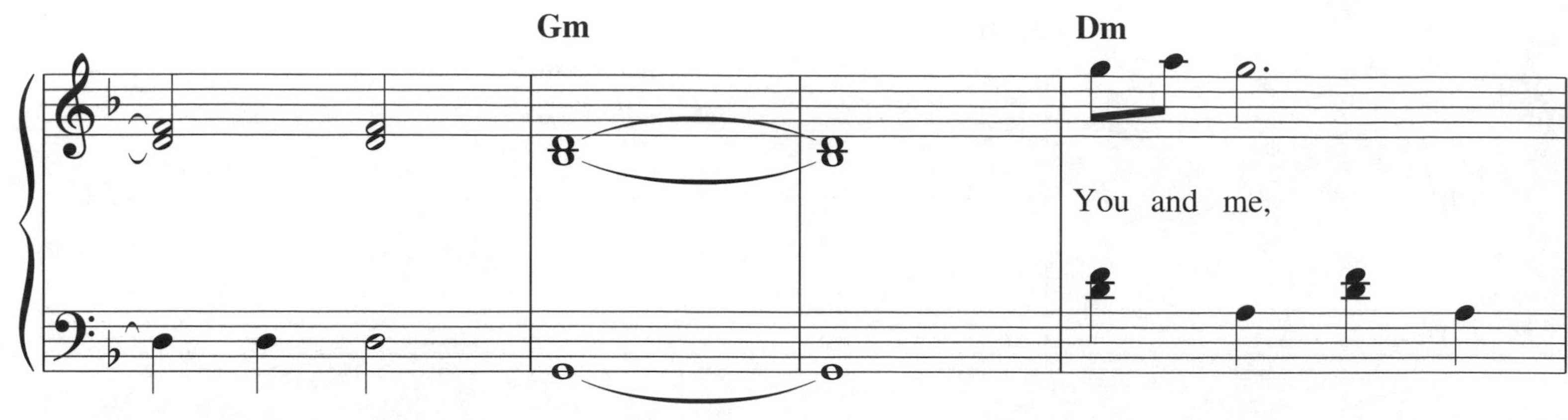
Gm
Dm
You and me,

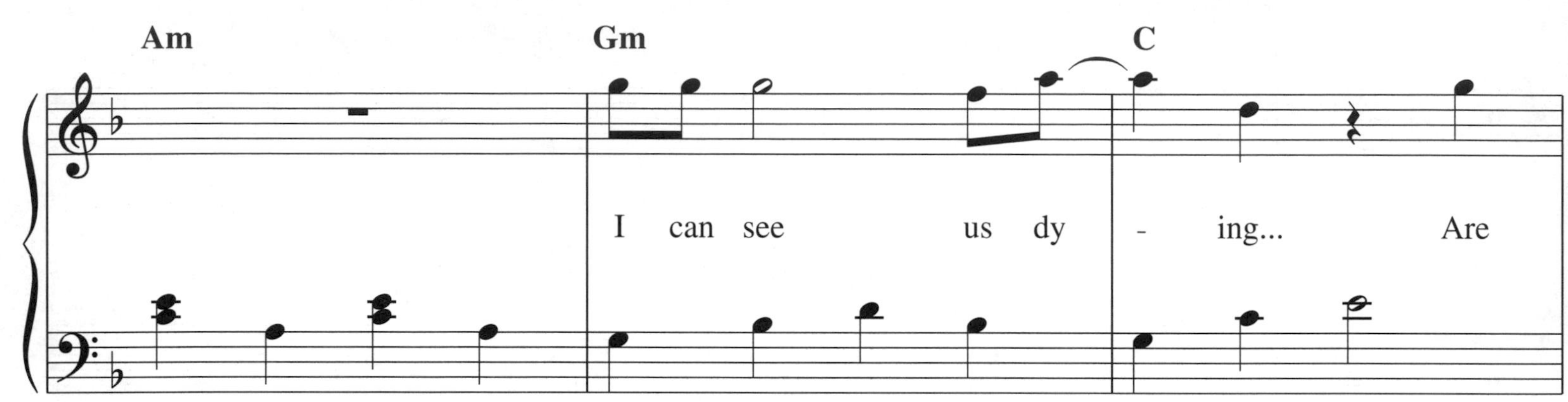
Am
Gm
C
I can see us dy - ing... Are

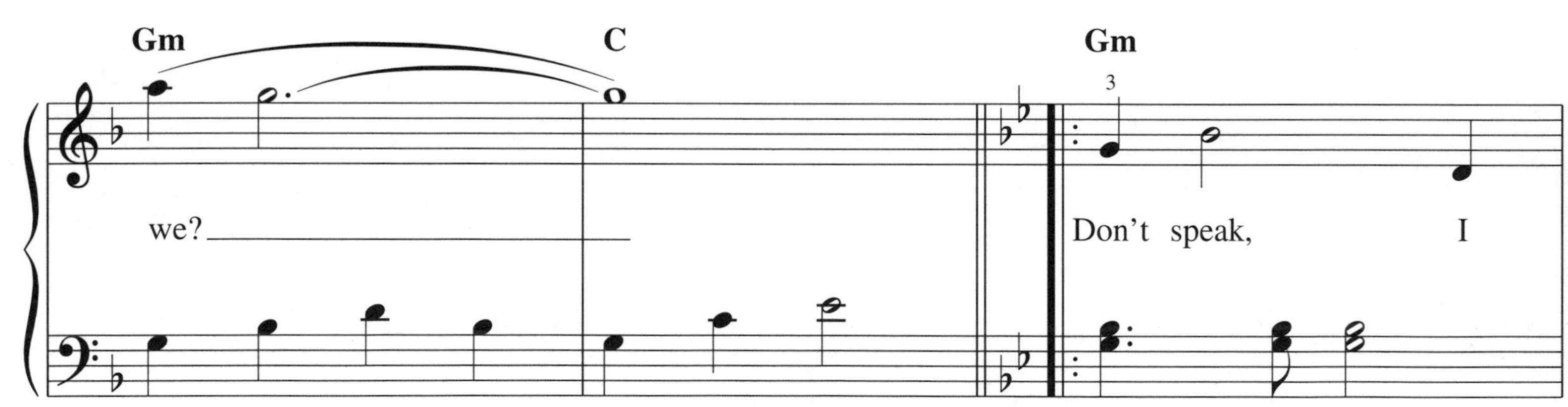
Gm
C
Gm
3
we?
Don't speak, I

Cm
F
D7
know just what you're say - ing,
so please stop ex - plain -

Cm
D7
Gm
- ing. Don't tell me 'cause it hurts.

Cm
D7
Gm
Cm
No, no, don't speak, I know what you're think -

F
D7
Cm
- ing. I don't need your rea - sons. Don't

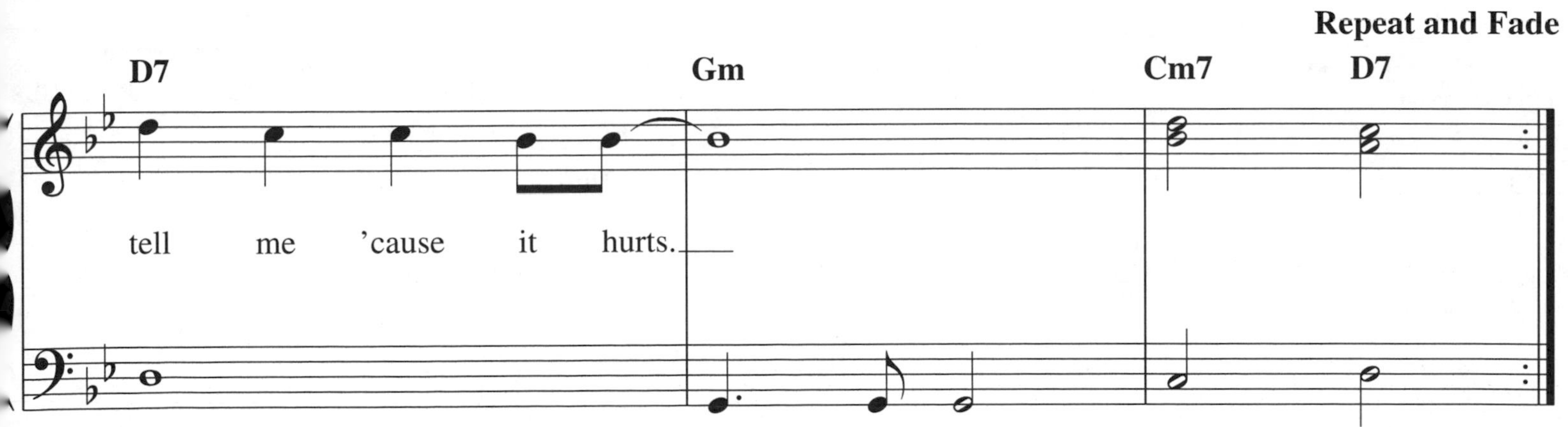

Repeat and Fade
D7
Gm
Cm7
D7
tell me 'cause it hurts.

CHANGE THE WORLD

featured on the Motion Picture Soundtrack PHENOMENON

Words and Music by GORDON KENNEDY,
TOMMY SIMS and WAYNE KIRKPATRICK

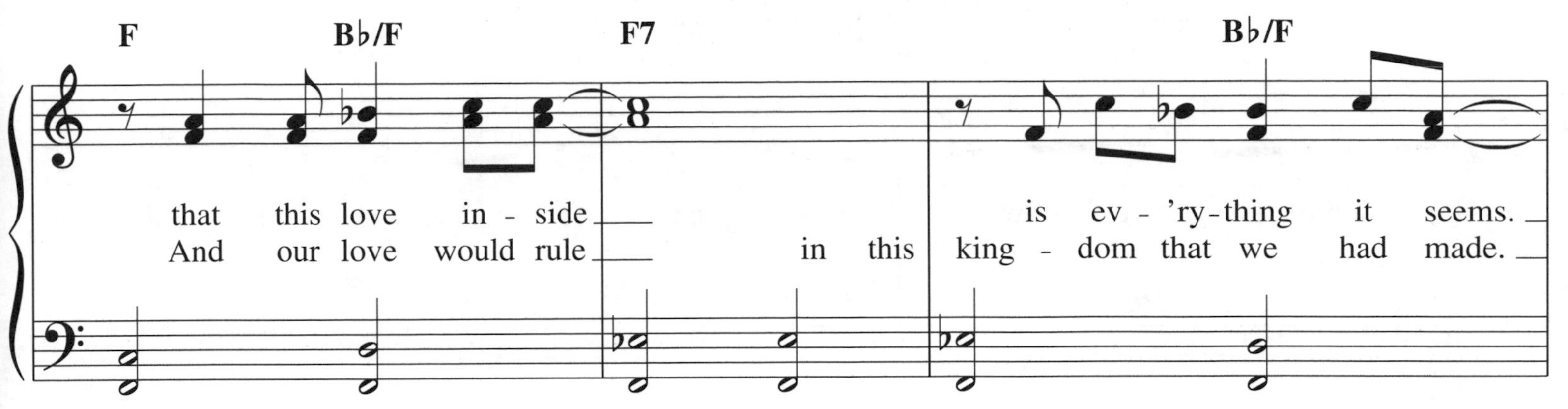
F
B♭/F
F7
B♭/F
that this love in - side
is ev - 'ry-thing it seems.
And our love would rule
in this
king - dom that we had made.

F
C
F/C
C7
But for now I find
Till then I'll be a fool,

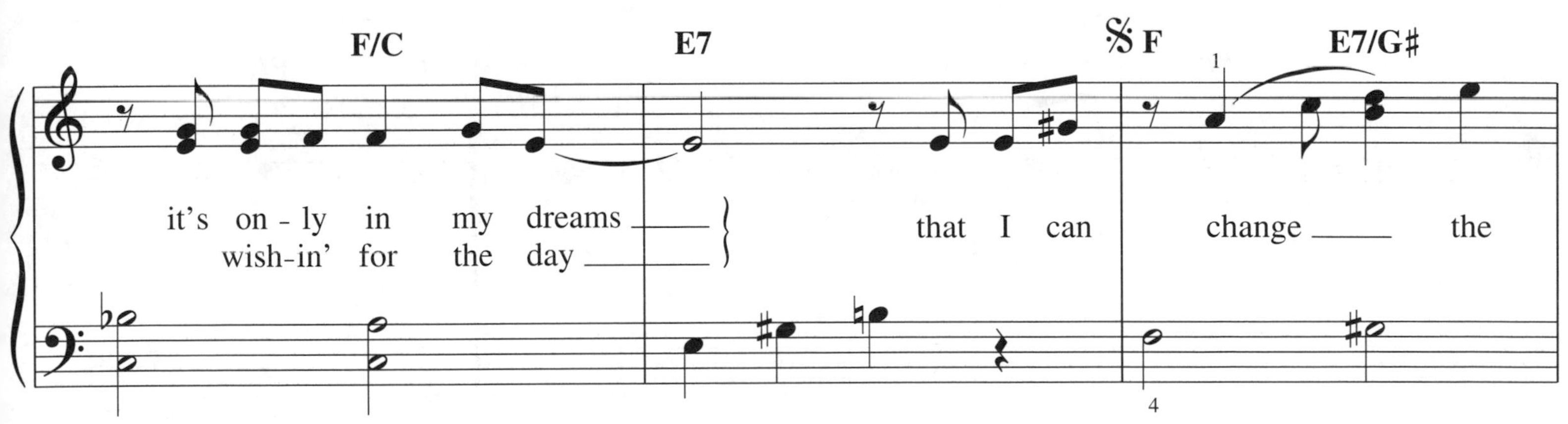
F/C
E7
F
E7/G♯
it's on - ly in my dreams
wish-in' for the day
that I can
change the

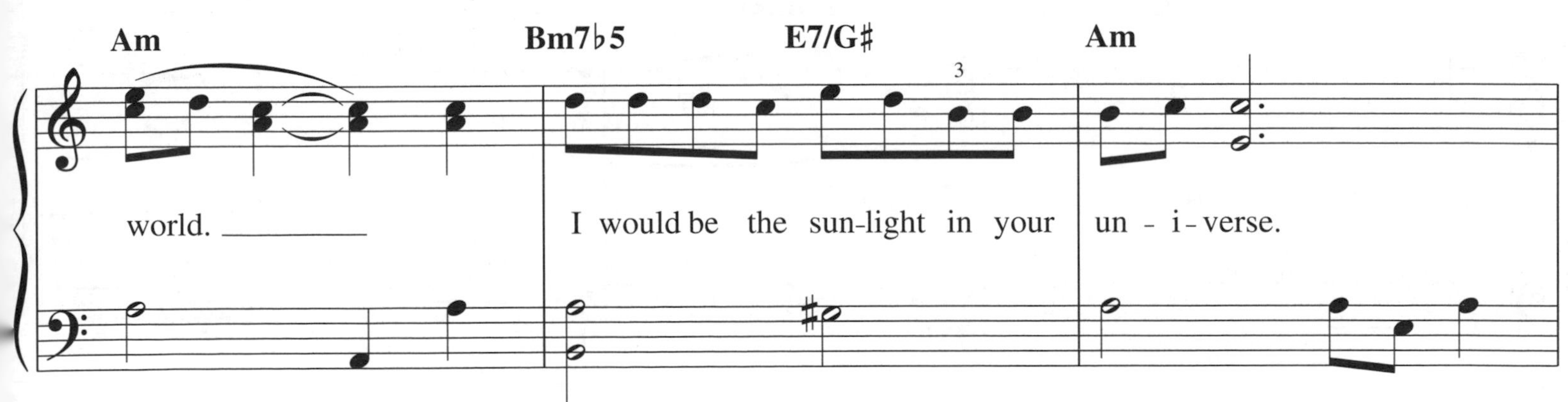
Am
Bm7♭5
E7/G♯
Am
world.
I would be the sun-light in your
un - i - verse.

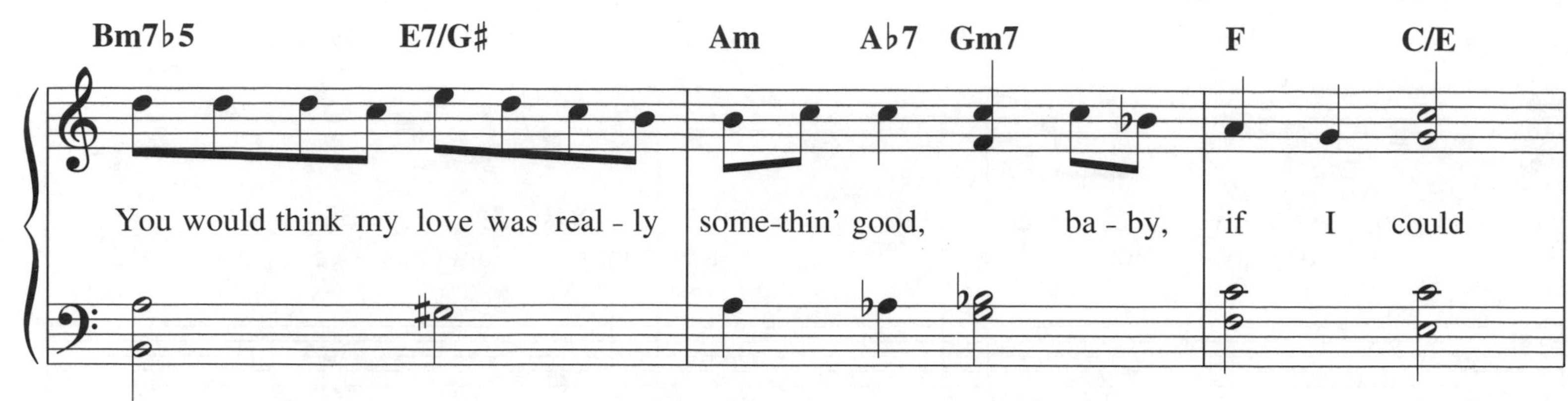
Bm7♭5
E7/G♯
Am
A♭7
Gm7
F
C/E
You would think my love was real - ly
some-thin' good,
ba - by,
if I could

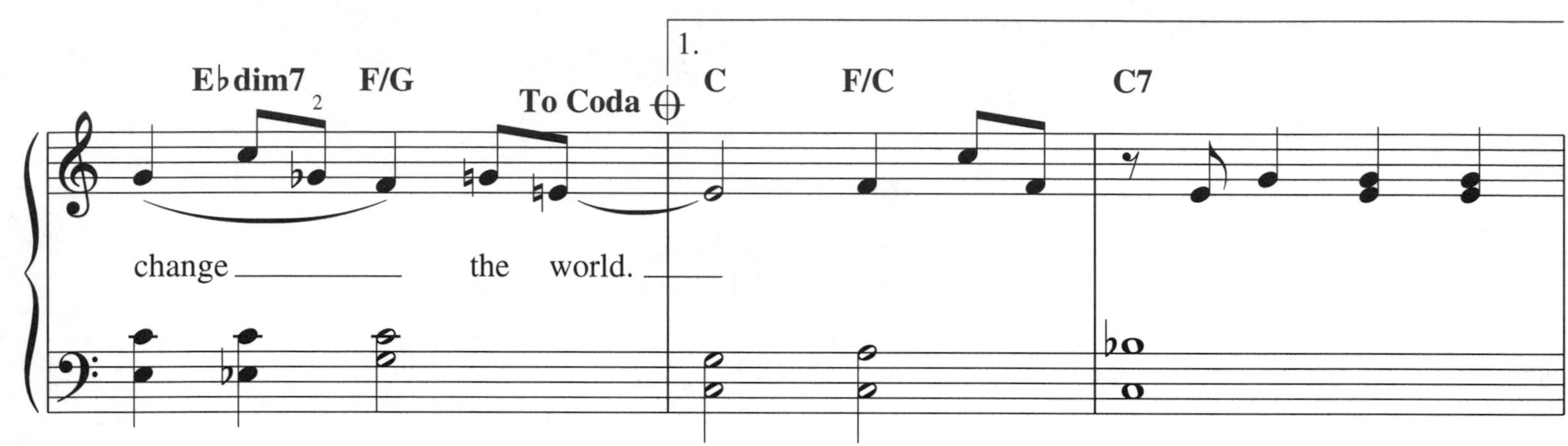
E♭dim7
F/G
To Coda
1.
C
F/C
C7
change
the world.

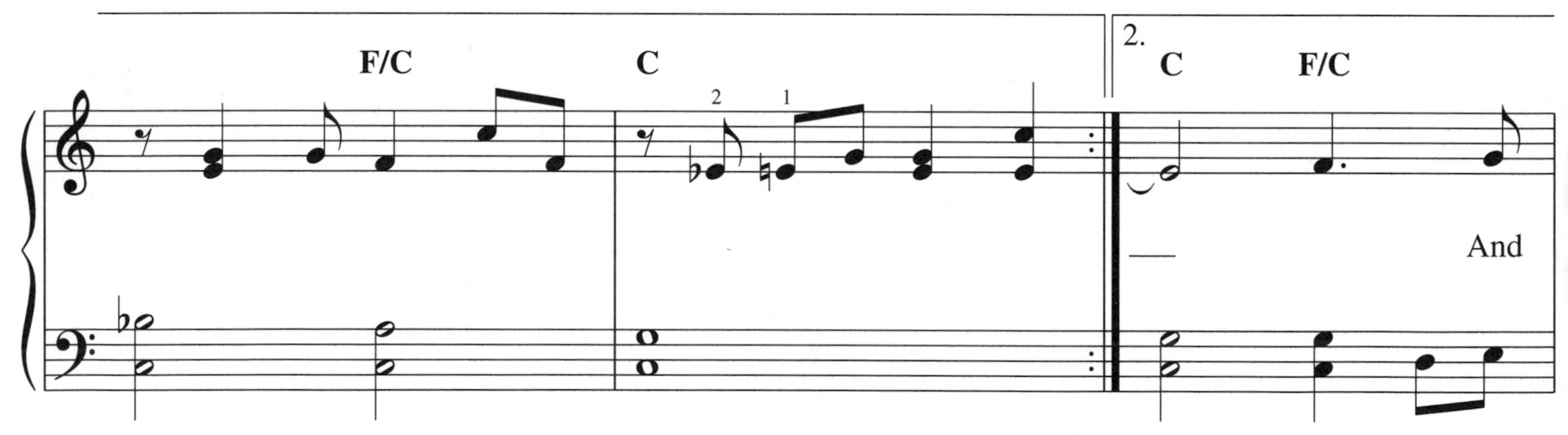
F/C
C
2.
C
F/C
And

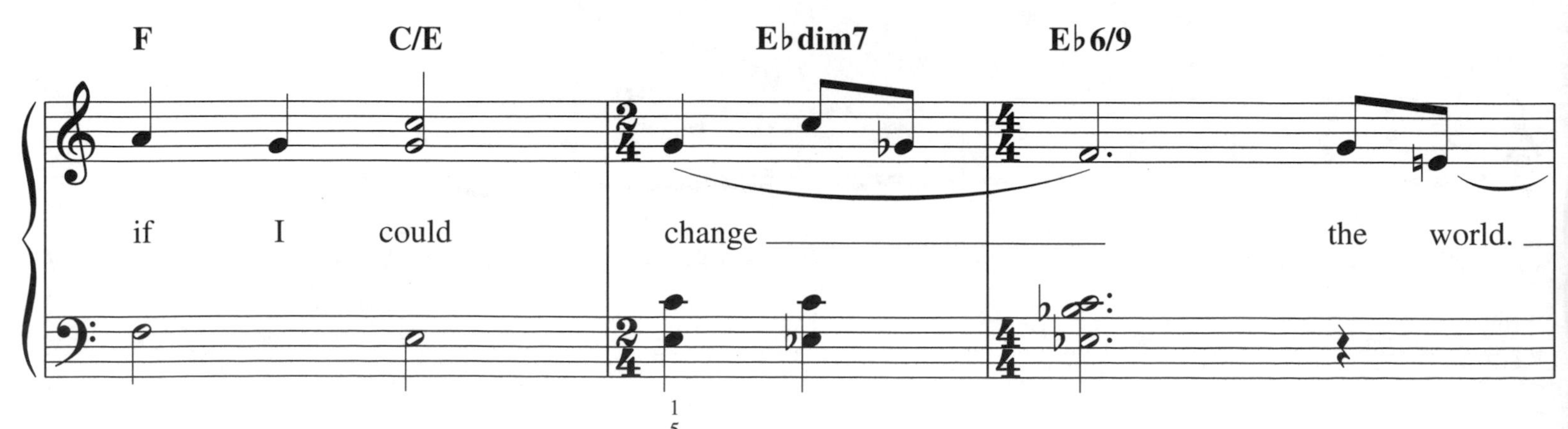
F
C/E
E♭dim7
E♭6/9
if I could
change
the world.

C
D
E♭
F
C
D
E♭
F
E
D.S. al Coda
I could
CODA
C
Ba - by,
F
C/E
E♭dim
E♭6/9
C
if I could change the world.

GROW OLD WITH ME

Words and Music by
JOHN LENNON

Em
Am7
D7
we will be as one.
when the day is done.
for our love is true.
C
Am7
G
Em
God bless our love,
C
D
G
D7
God bless our love.
To Coda
G
1.
2.
G
Grow

Gmaj7 Em7 Bm/D

Spend-ing our lives to - geth - er

Em7 Bm/D

man and wife to - geth - er,

C Am7 Gsus G

world with - out end, ___ world with - out end. ___

D.S. al Coda

CODA

G G+ C G

rit.

p

FORREST GUMP - MAIN TITLE

(Feather Theme)

from the Paramount Motion Picture FORREST GUMP

Music by ALAN SILVESTRI

Em
C
Am
D/F#
G
C/G

Am
D/F♯
G
Em
C
Am
D/F♯
G

molto cresc.
C
f
F/C
Dm
G
C
Am

F
Dm
G
C
dim.
mp
fading away
rit.
ppp

HERO

Words and Music by MARIAH CAREY
and WALTER AFANASIEFF

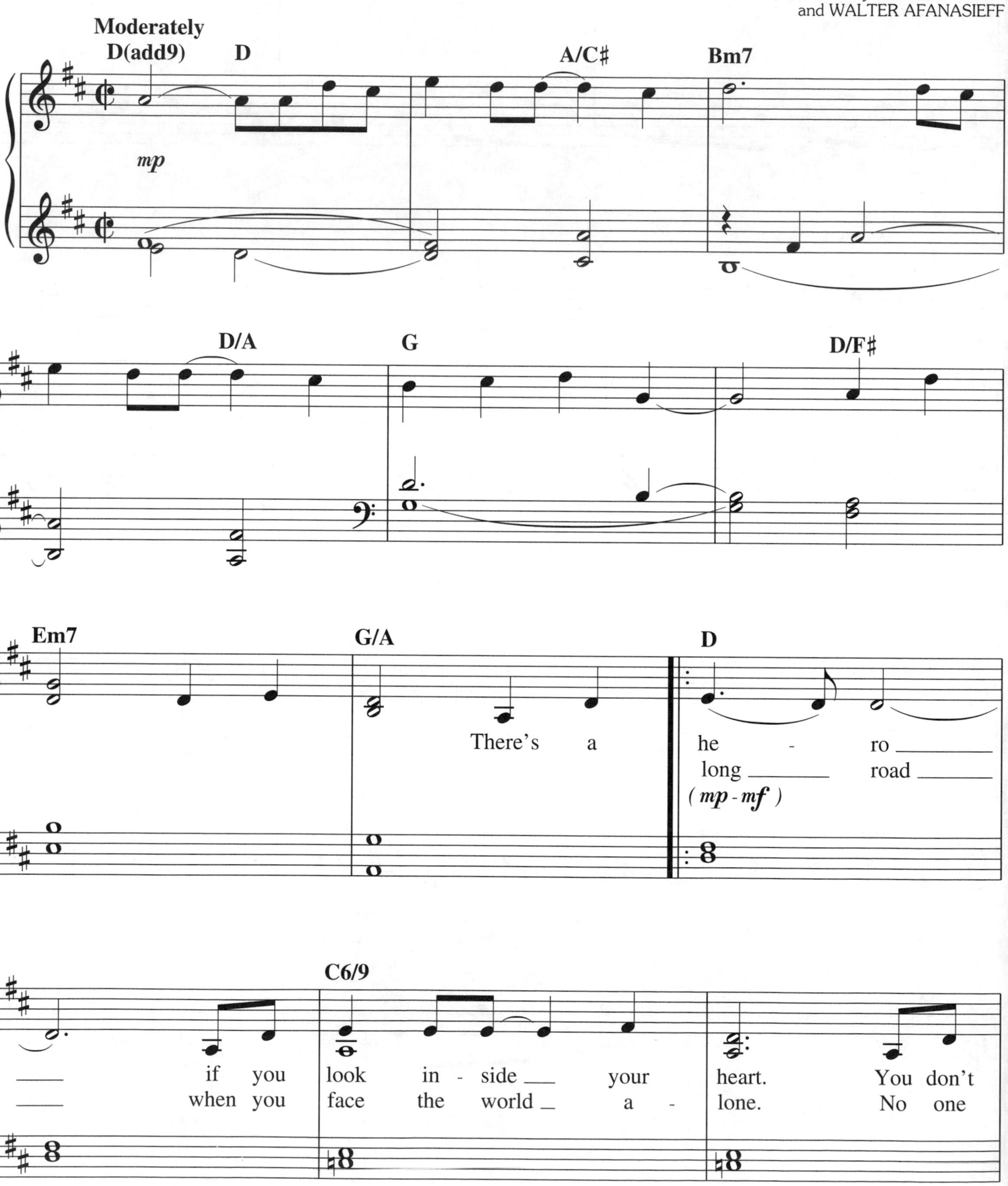
Moderately
D(add9)
D
A/C♯
Bm7
mp
D/A
G
D/F♯
Em7
G/A
D
There's a
he - ro
long road
(mp - mf)
C6/9
if you
when you
look in - side your
face the world a -
heart. You don't
lone. No one

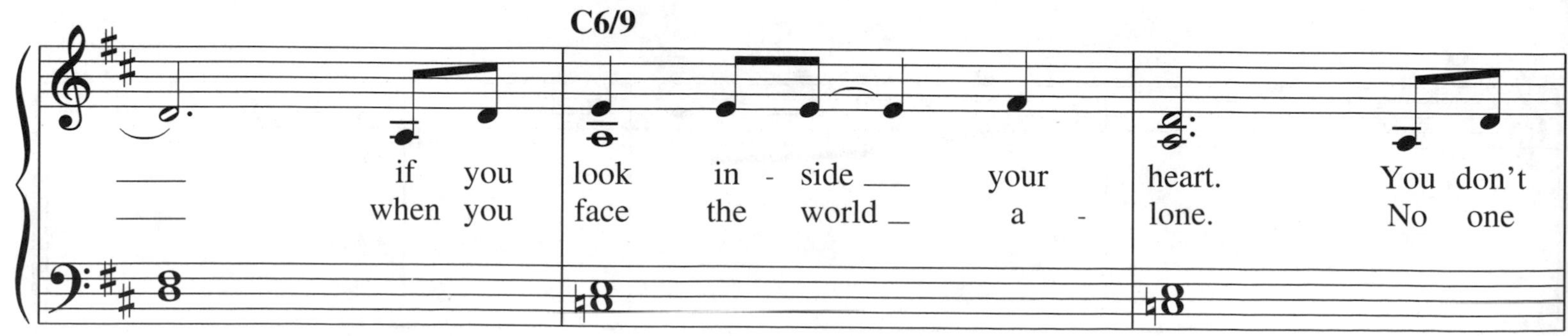

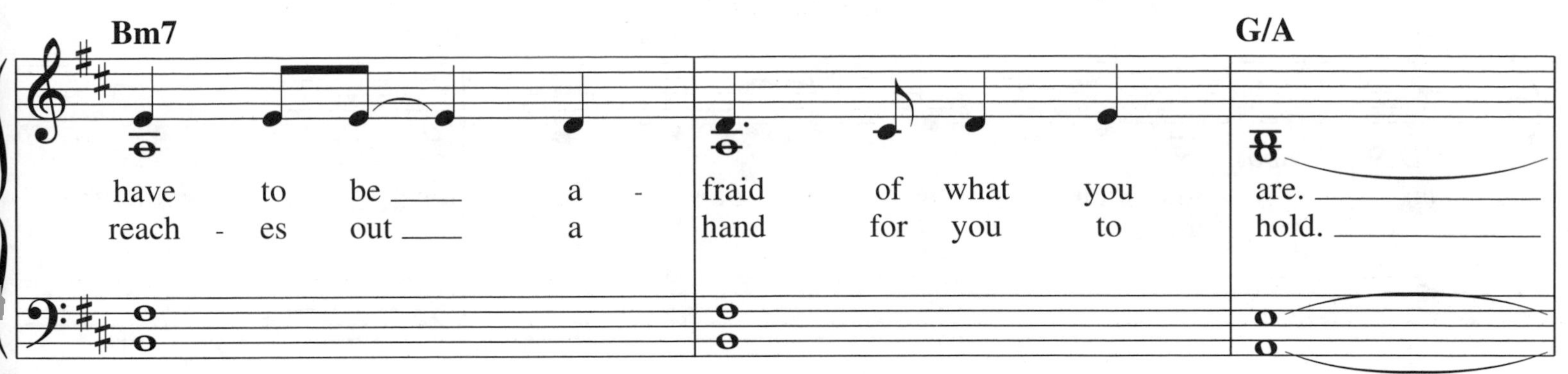
Bm7
G/A
have to be a - fraid of what you are.
reach - es out a hand for you to hold.

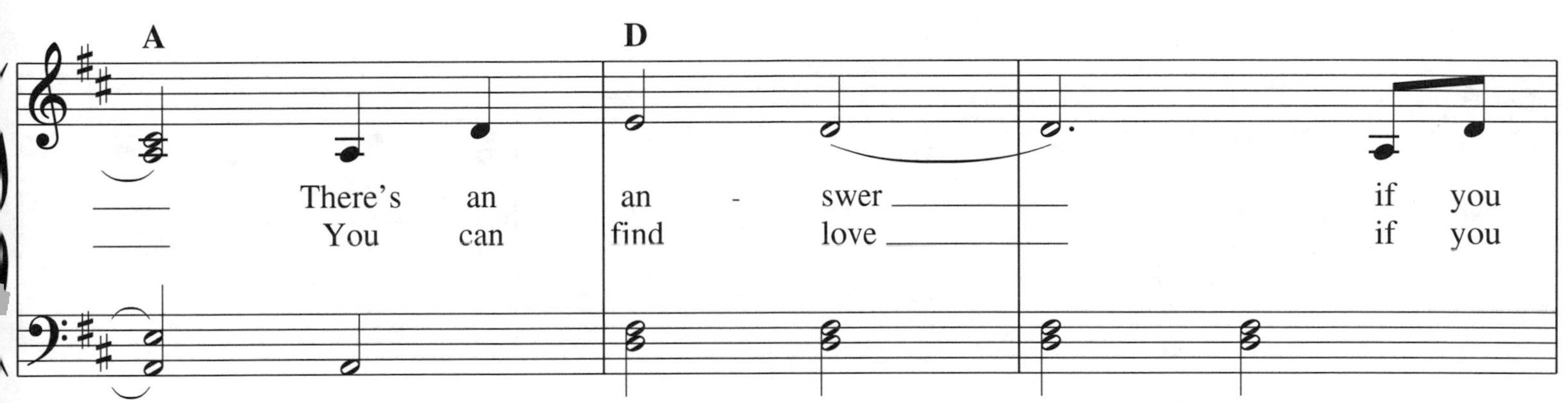
A
D
There's an an - swer if you
You can find love if you

C/E
B♭(add9)
reach in - to your soul and the sor - row that you
search with - in your - self and the emp - ti - ness you

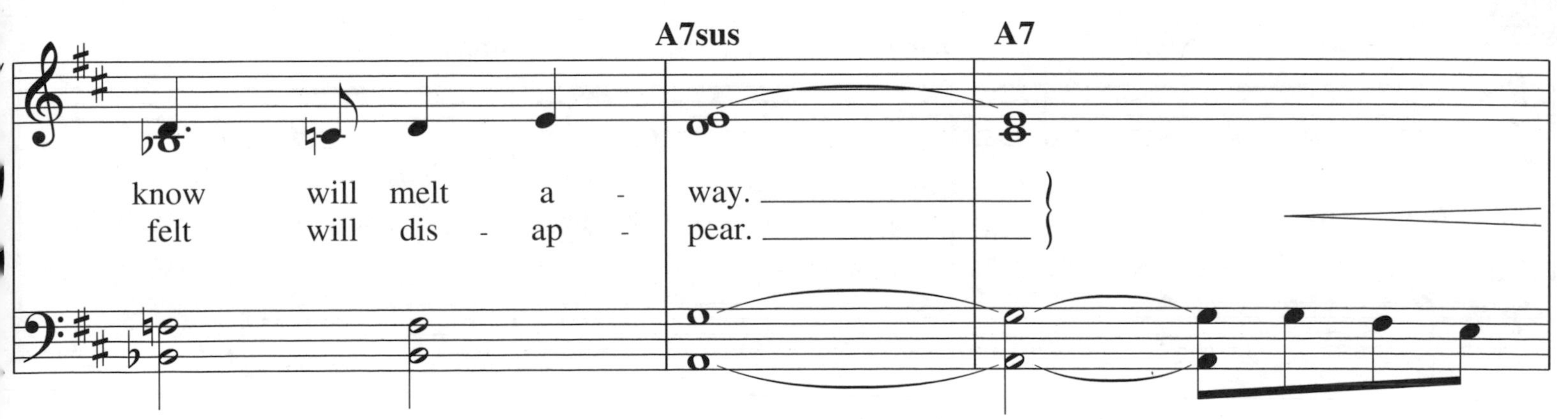
A7sus
A7
know will melt a - way.
felt will dis - ap - pear.

D
A/C♯
Bm7
(D.S. a tempo)
mf
And then a he - ro comes a - long with the

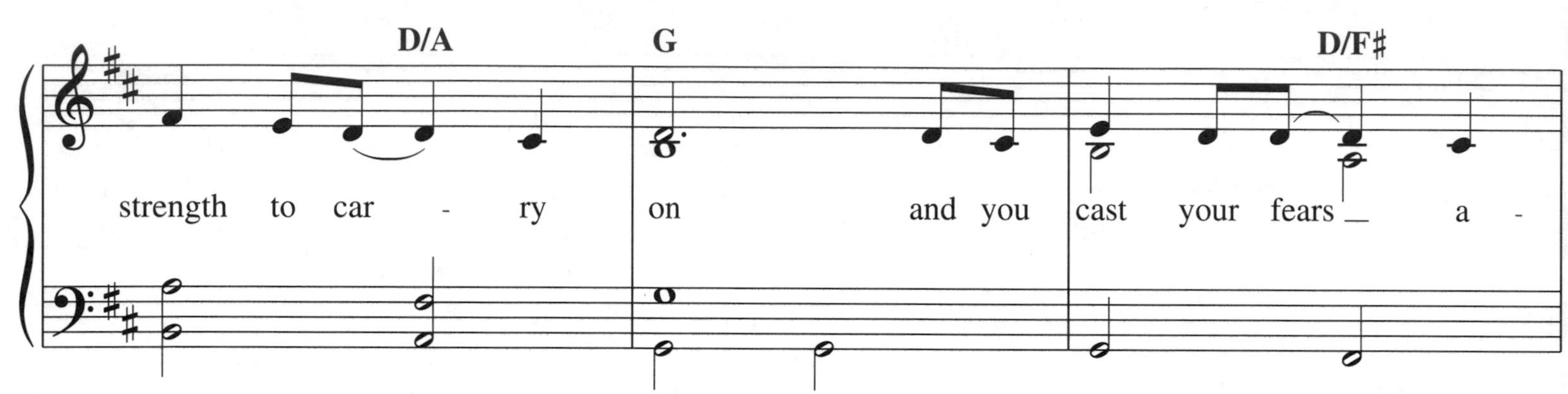
D/A
G
D/F♯
strength to car - ry on and you cast your fears a -

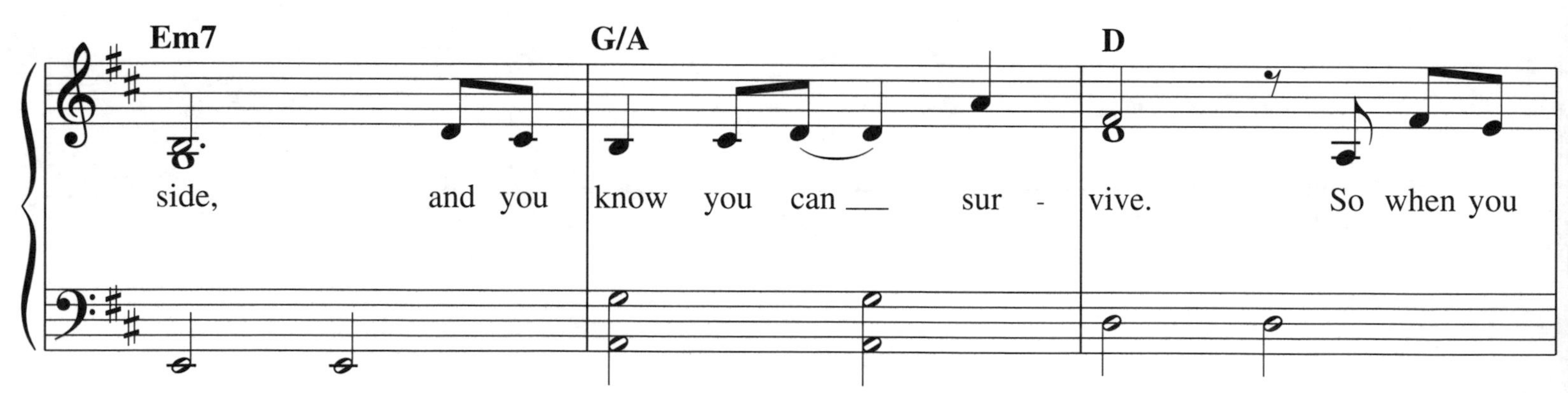
Em7
G/A
D
side, and you know you can sur - vive. So when you

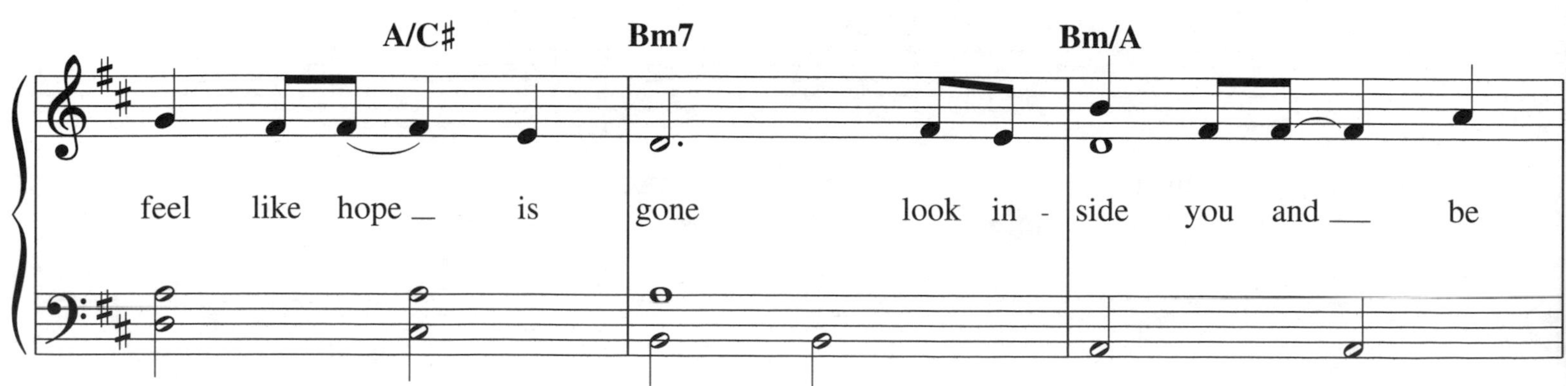
A/C♯
Bm7
Bm/A
feel like hope is gone look in - side you and be

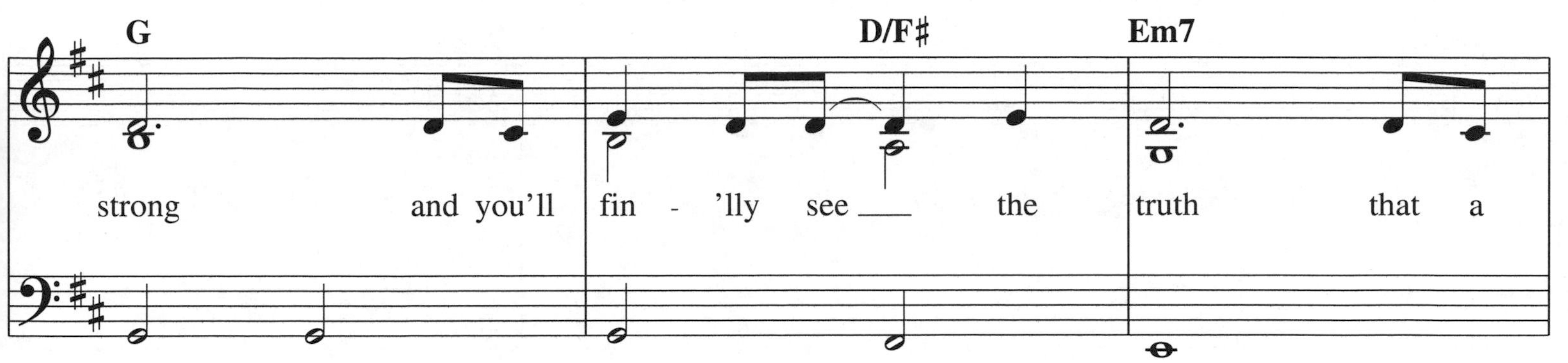
G
D/F♯
Em7
strong and you'll fin - 'lly see the truth that a

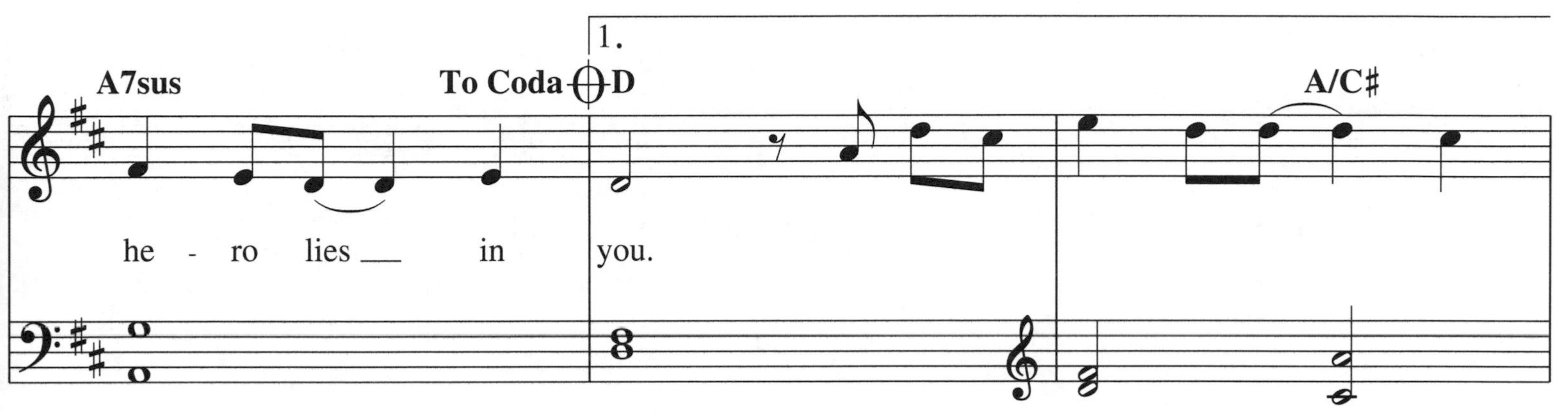
A7sus
To Coda
D
1.
A/C♯
he - ro lies in you.

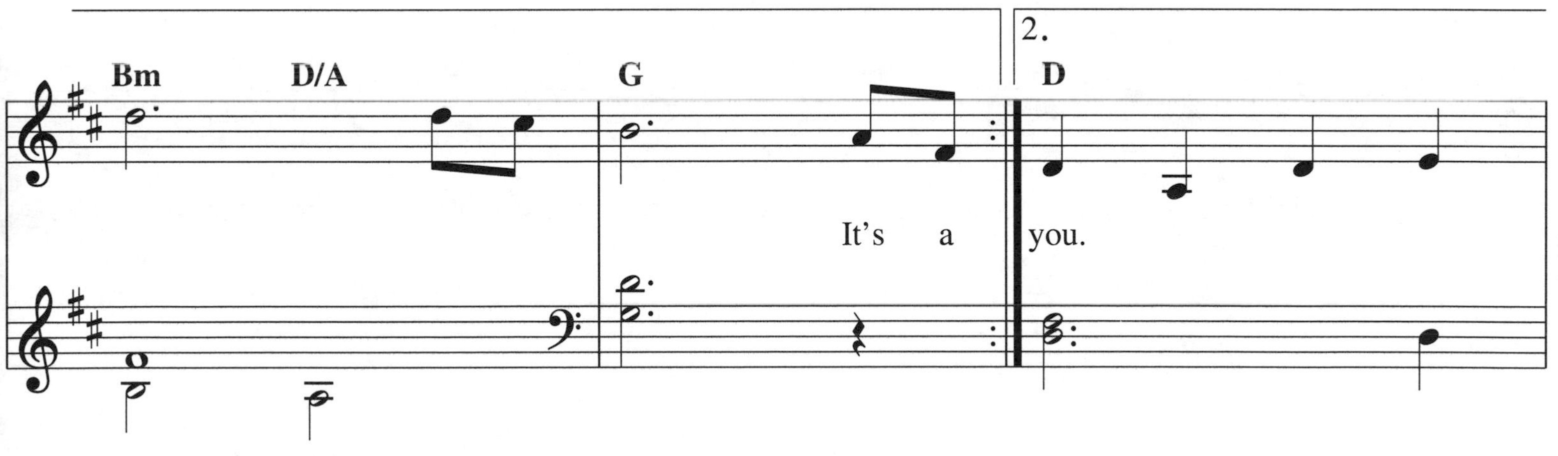
Bm
D/A
G
2.
D
It's a you.

B♭
F/A
Lord knows

F
C
B♭
dreams are hard to fol - low, but don't let

F/A
F
C/E
Dm7
C
an - y - one tear them a - way.

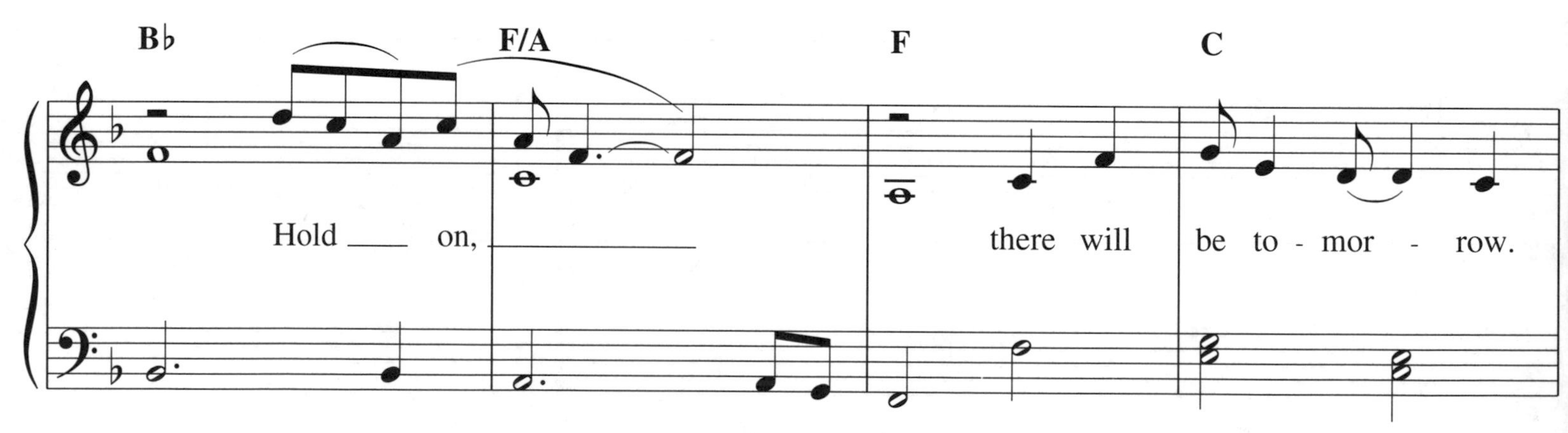
B♭
F/A
F
C
Hold on, there will be to - mor - row.

D.S. al Coda
B♭
F/A
3
G/A
A
In time you'll find the way.
rall.

CODA
G
D/F#
Em7
you.
That a
molto rall.

A7sus
A7
D
A/C#
he - ro lies in
you.
mp a tempo

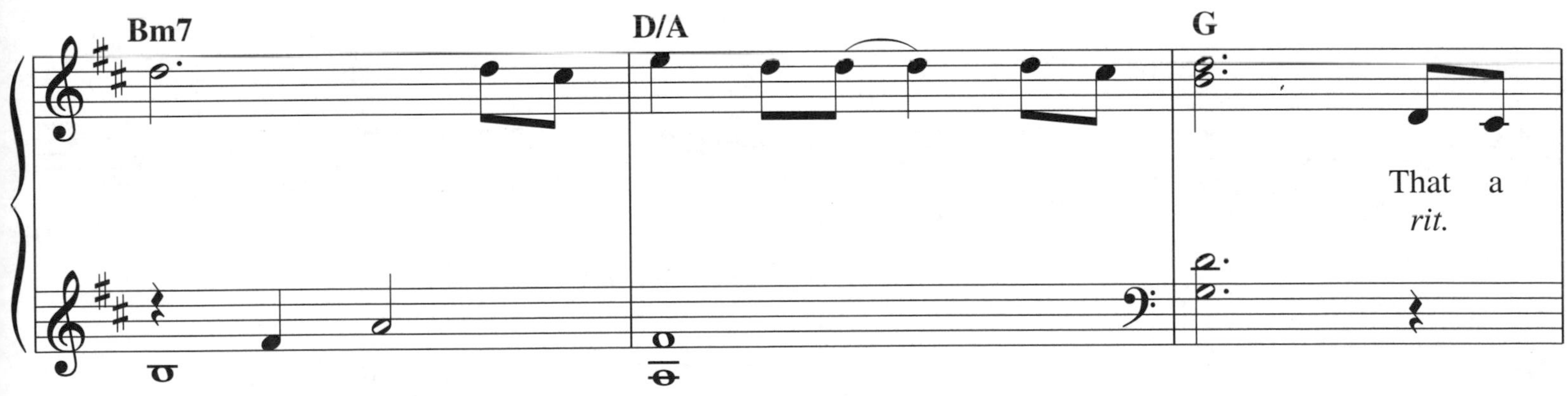
Bm7
D/A
G
That a
rit.

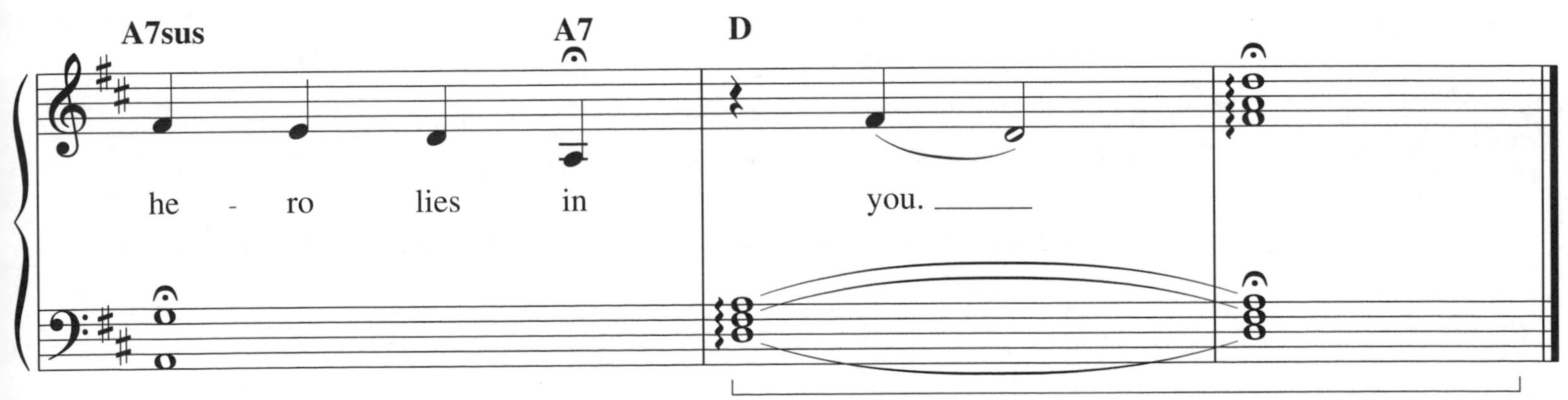
A7sus
A7
D
he - ro lies in
you.

IT'S ALL COMING BACK TO ME NOW

Words and Music by
JIM STEINMAN

Moderately, with feeling

F C/G G Em Am
ev - er.
I fin - ished cry - ing in the
Thought you were his - t'ry with the
F G7 C Em Am F Gsus G
in - stant that you left, and I can't re - mem - ber where or when or how. And I
slam - ming of the door, and I made my - self so strong a - gain some - how. And I
Em Am F G F
ban - ished ev - 'ry mem - 'ry you and I had ev - er made.
nev - er was - ted an - y of my time on you since then.
rit.
F/G C G/B
But when you touch me like this, and you hold me like that, I just
But if I touch you like this, and if you kiss me like that, it was
a tempo

Am Dm F G7
have to ad - mit that it's all com - ing back to me. When I
so long a - go but it's all com - ing back to me. If you

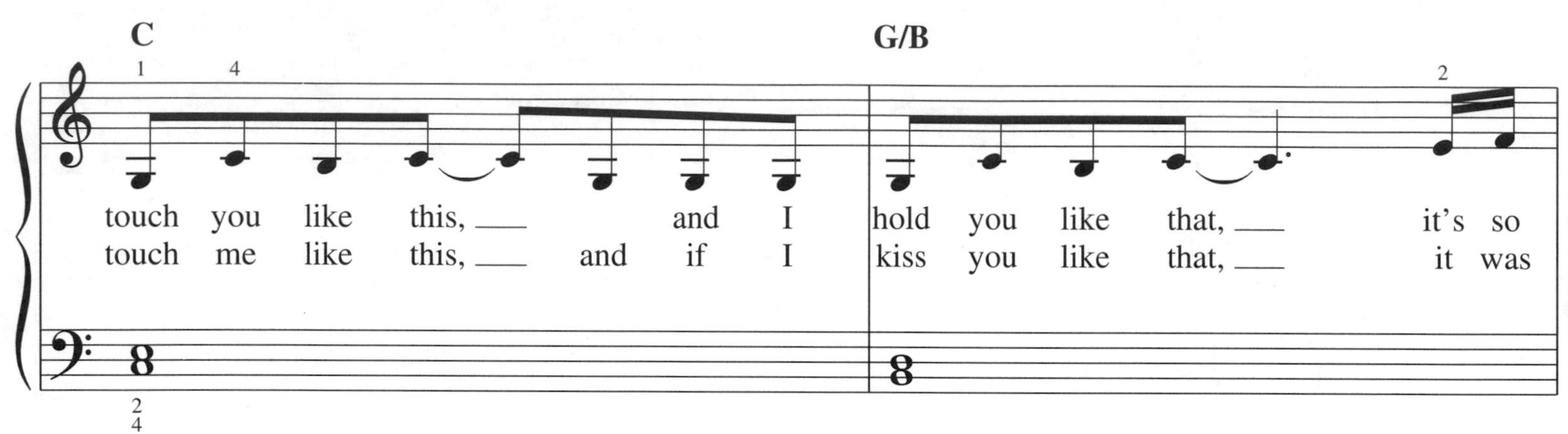
C G/B
touch you like this, and I hold you like that, it's so
touch me like this, and if I kiss you like that, it was

Am7 Dm F G7
hard to be - lieve, but it's all com - ing back to me.
gone with the wind, but it's all com - ing back to me.
It's

C F G
all com - ing back, it's all com - ing back to me now. There were

Am7
F
Em
F
mo - ments of gold ___ and there were flash - es of light. ___ There were

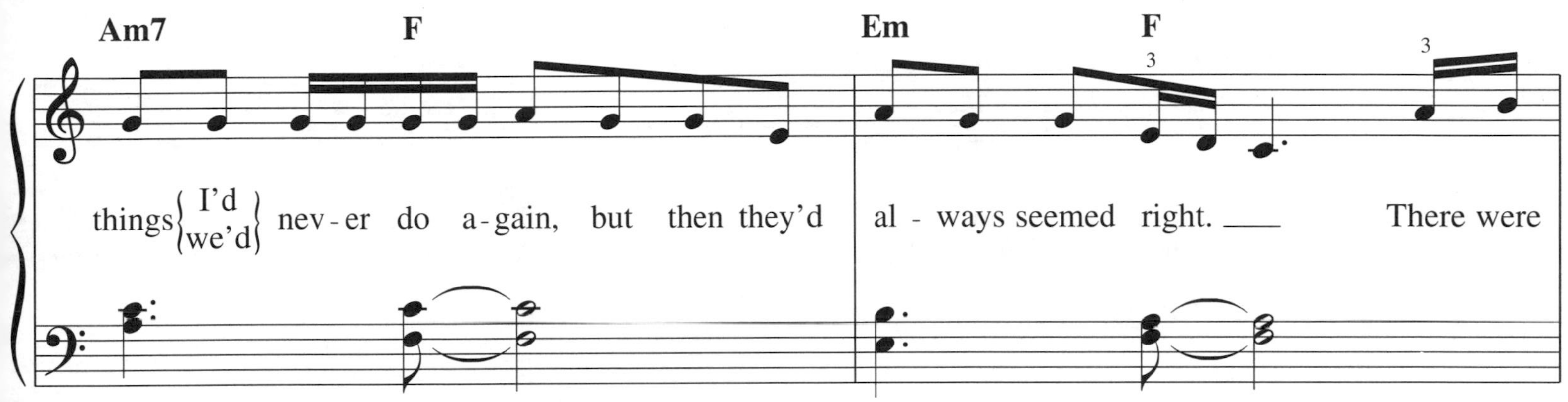
Am7
F
Em
F
things I'd / we'd nev - er do a - gain, but then they'd al - ways seemed right. ___ There were

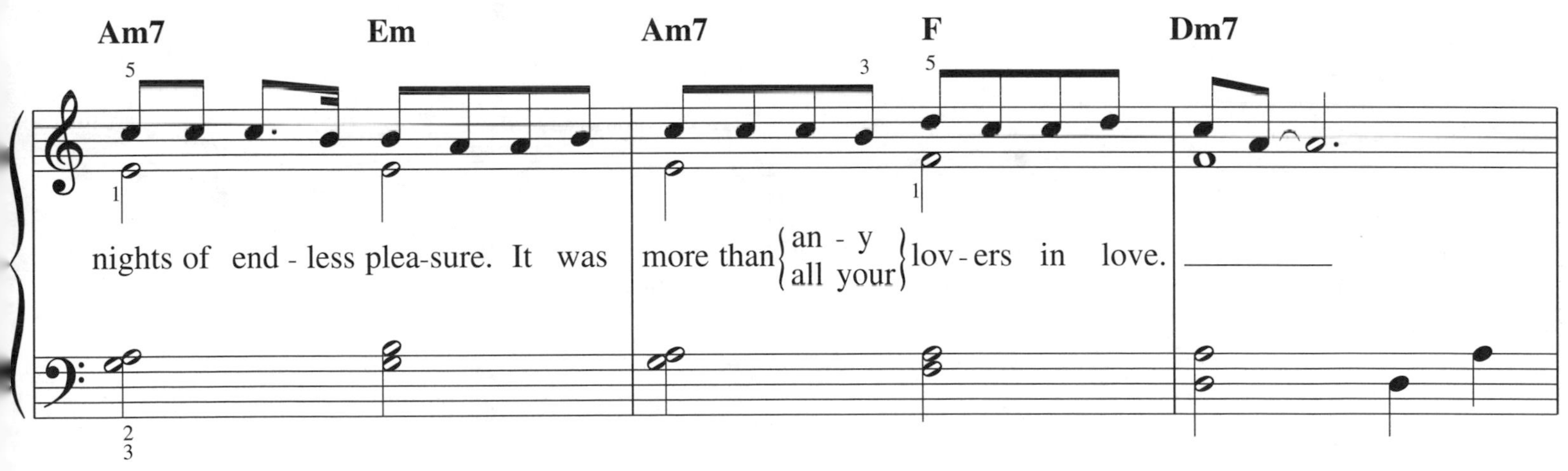
Am7
Em
Am7
F
Dm7
nights of end - less plea - sure. It was more than an - y / all your lov - ers in love. ___

F/G
C
G/B
Ba - by, ba - by, if I kiss you like this, _ and if you whis - per like that, _ it was
Ba - by, ba - by, when you touch me like this, _ and when you hold me like that, _ it was

Am7 Dm F G7
lost long a - go, but it's all com - ing back to me. If you
gone with the wind, but it's all com - ing back to me. When you
C G/B
want me like this, and if you need me like that, it was
see me like this, and when I see you like that, then we've

Am7 Dm F G7
that long a - go, but it's all com - ing back to me. It's so
seen what we want, to see all com - ing back to me. The

Am7 Dm F G7
hard to re - sist, and it's all com - ing back to me.
flesh and the fan - ta - sies all com - ing back to me.
I can

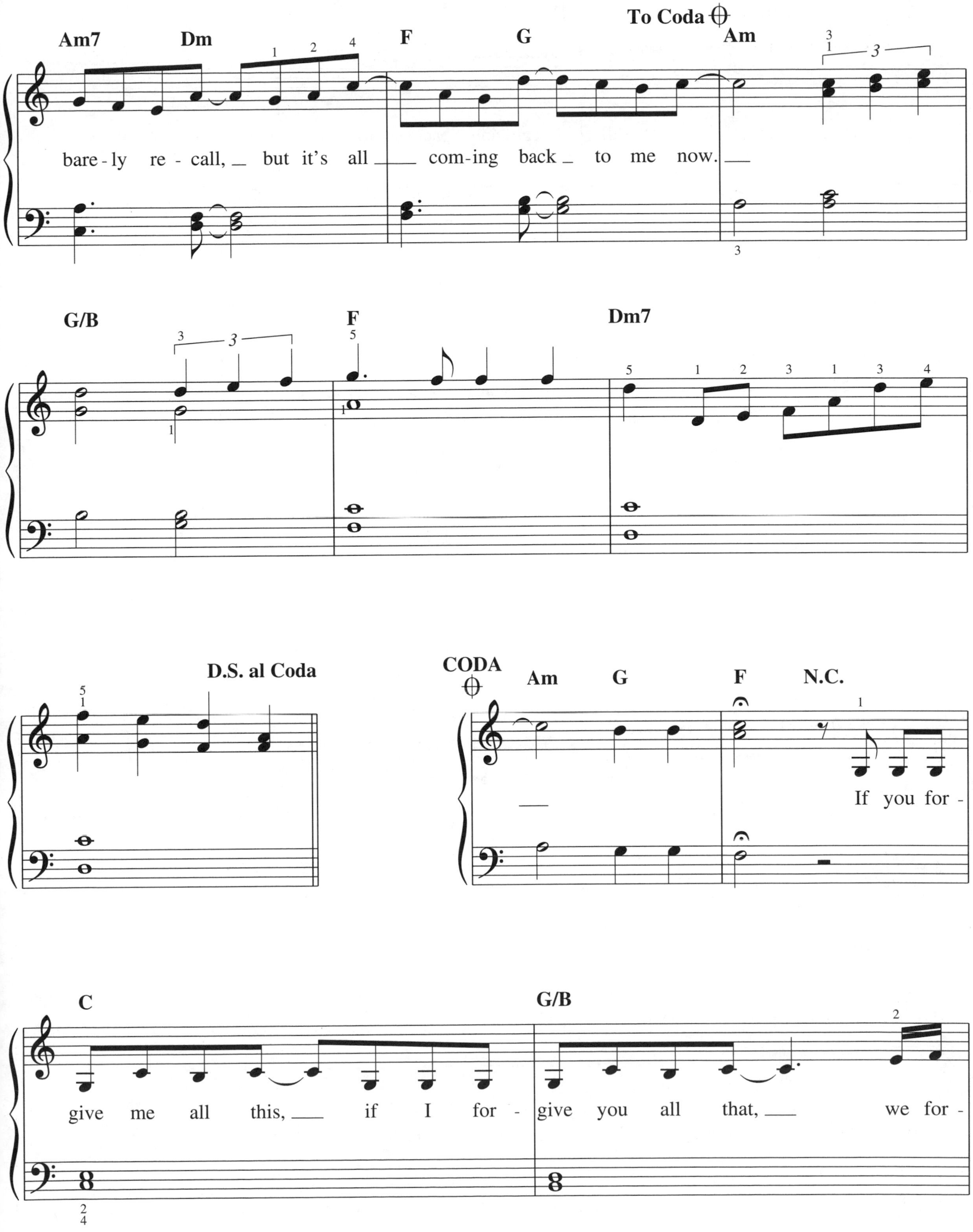

To Coda 𝄌

Am7 Dm F G Am

bare-ly re-call, but it's all coming back to me now.

G/B F Dm7

D.S. al Coda

CODA

Am G F N.C.

If you for-

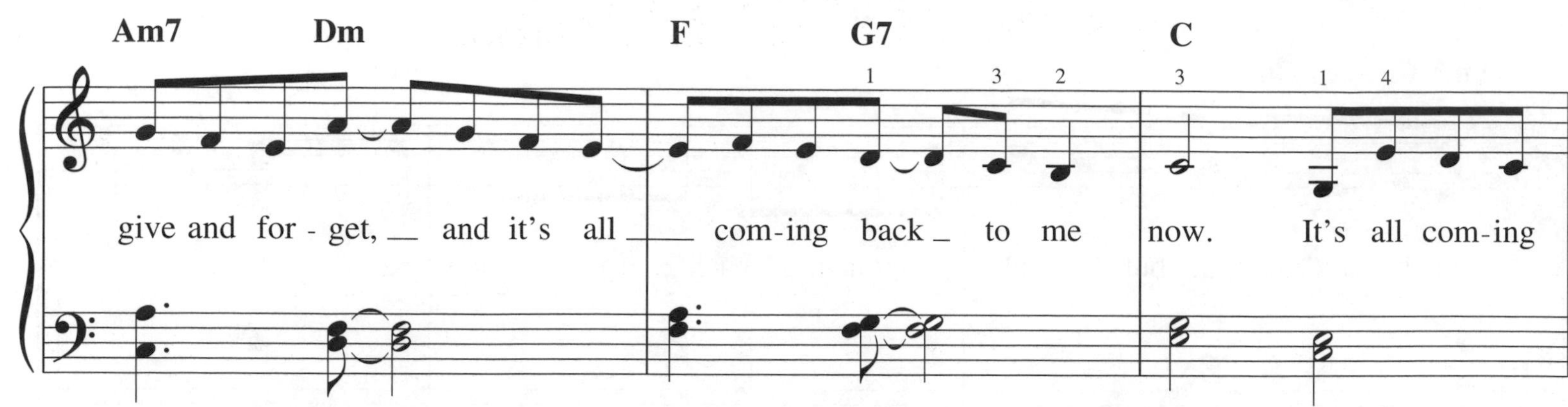
Am7
Dm
F
G7
C
give and for - get, and it's all com-ing back to me now. It's all com-ing

F
G
C
back to me now. And when I touch you like that, it's all com-ing

F
G
C
back to me now. And if you do it like this, it's all com-ing

F
C
back to me now. And if we...
rit.

IT'S YOUR LOVE

Words and Music by
STEPHONY E. SMITH

D
G
Oh, it's a beau - ti - ful thing.
Don't think I can
D
Em
C
keep it all in.
I just got - ta let you know
D
what it is that won't let me go.
Both: It's your
G
D
love.
It just does some - thin' to me.

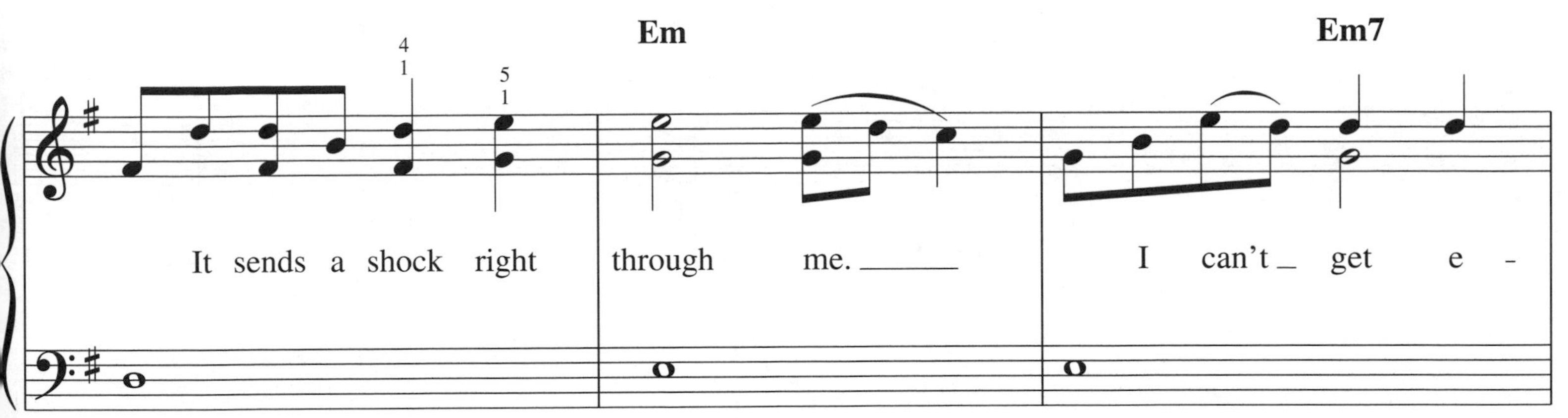
Em
Em7
It sends a shock right through me.
I can't get e -

C
G
nough.
And if you won - der

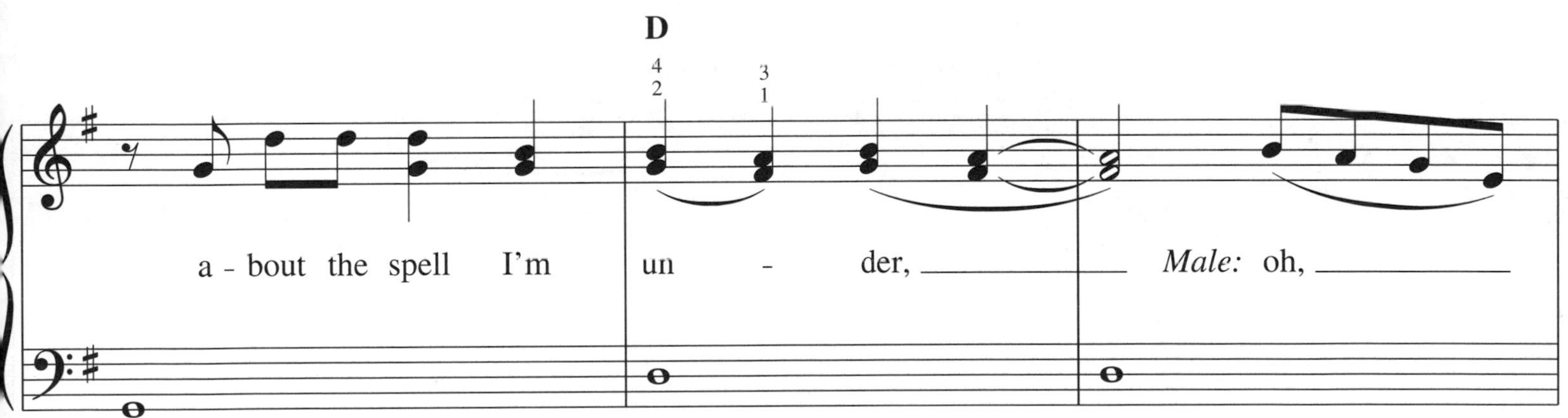
D
a - bout the spell I'm un - der,
Male: oh,

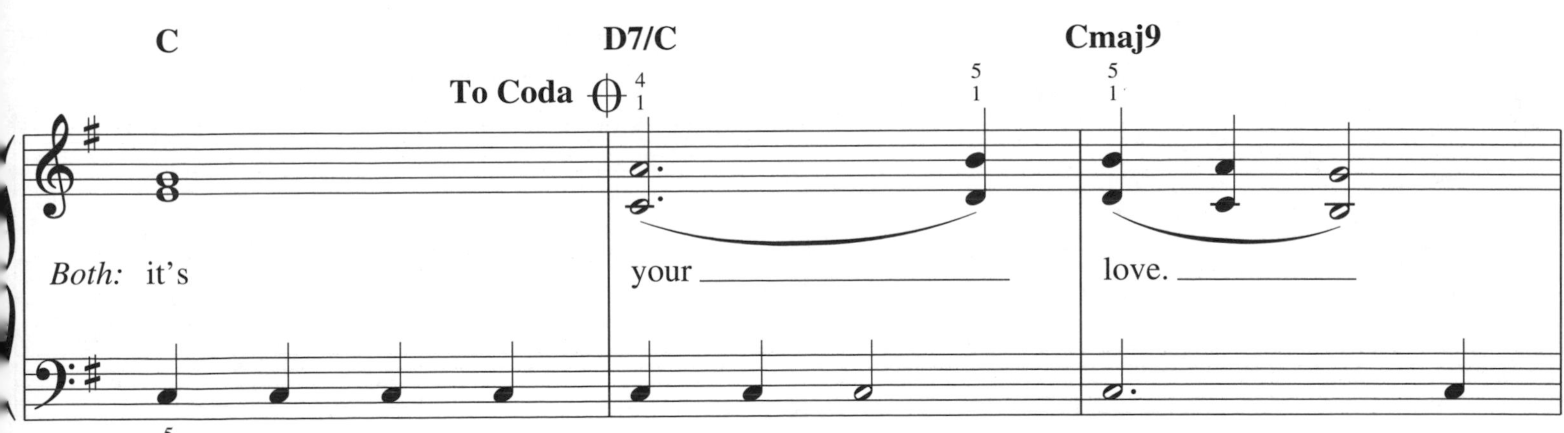
C
D7/C
Cmaj9
To Coda
Both: it's your love.

C
G
D/F♯
Male: Bet - ter than I was
more than I am

Em7
C
and all of this hap - pened
by tak-in' your hand.

D
G
And who I am now
is who I

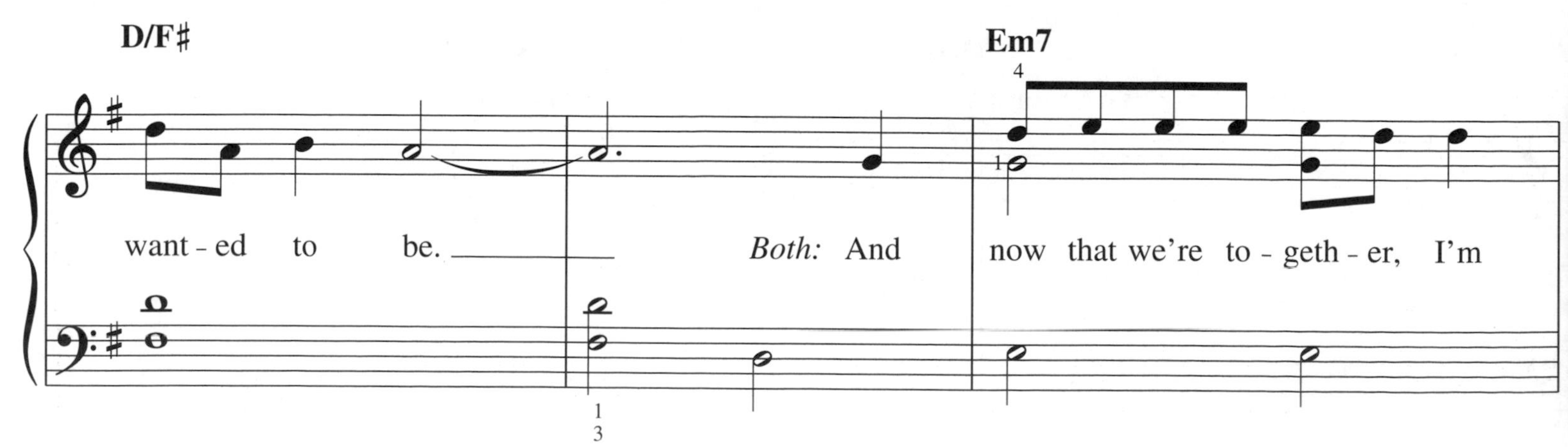
D/F♯
Em7
want - ed to be.
Both: And now that we're to - geth - er, I'm

C
D.S. al Coda
strong - er than ev - er. I'm
hap - py and free.
Oh, it's a

CODA
D7/C
Cmaj9
C
your
love.
Whoa.
It's

D7/C
Cmaj9
C
your
love.
It's
mp
rit.

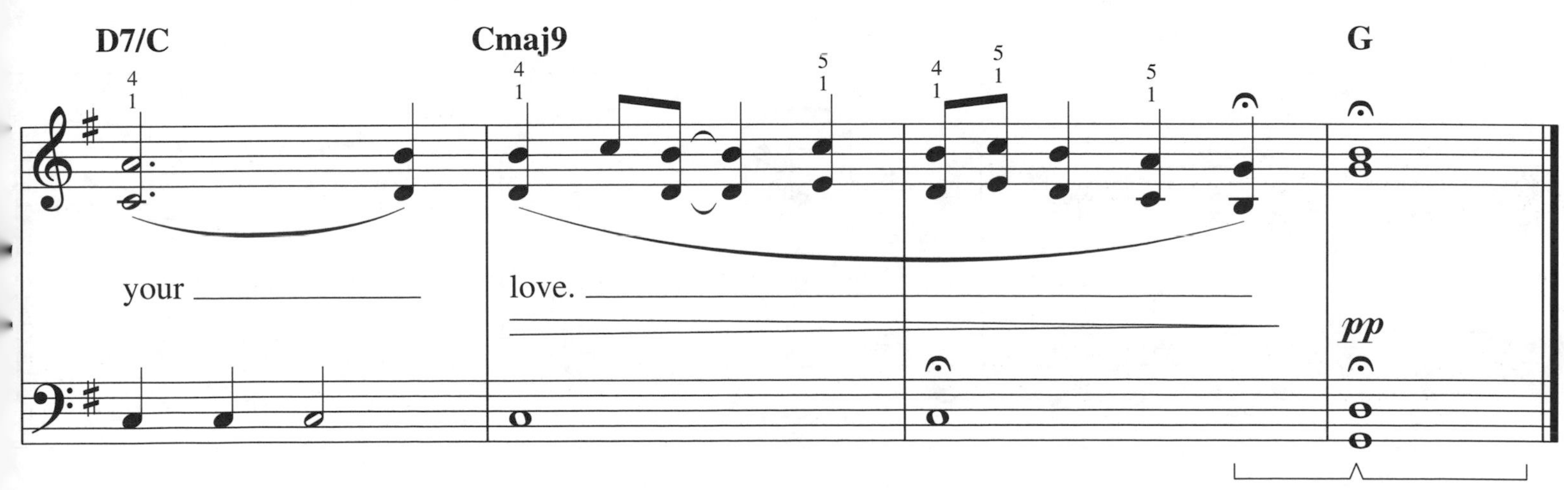
D7/C
Cmaj9
G
your
love.
pp

MISSION: IMPOSSIBLE THEME

from the Paramount Motion Picture MISSION: IMPOSSIBLE

By LALO SCHIFRIN

ff

MY HEART WILL GO ON

(Love Theme from 'Titanic')

from the Paramount and Twentieth Century Fox Motion Picture TITANIC

Music by JAMES HORNER
Lyric by WILL JENNINGS

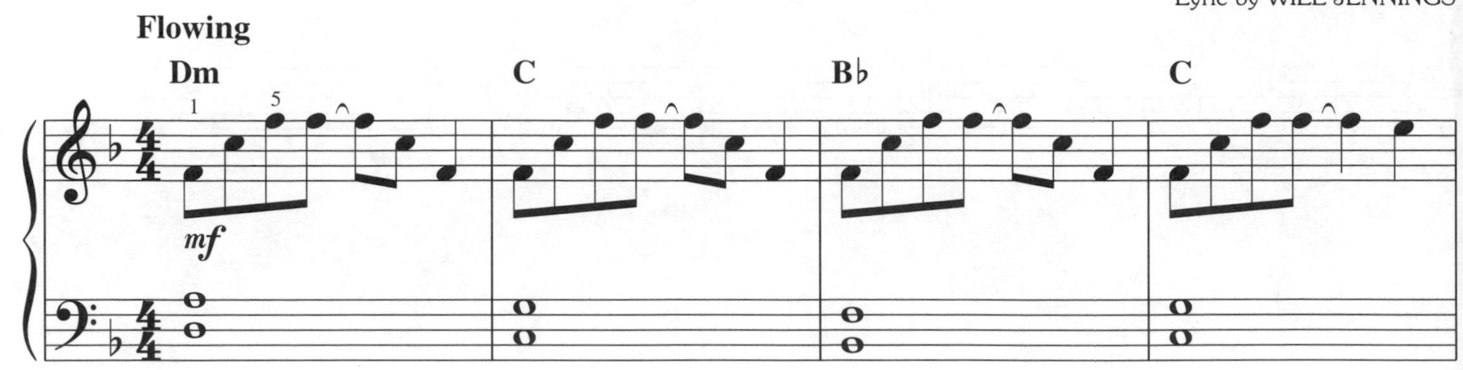

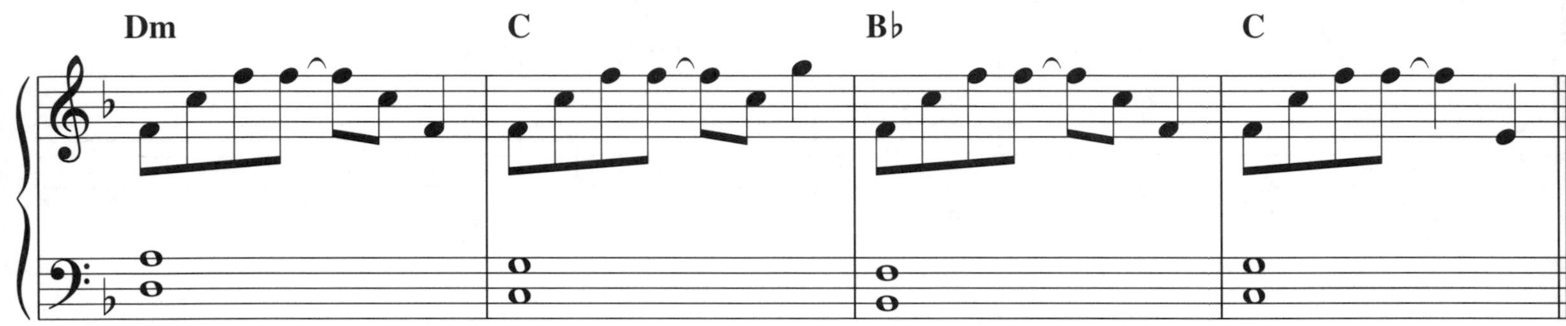

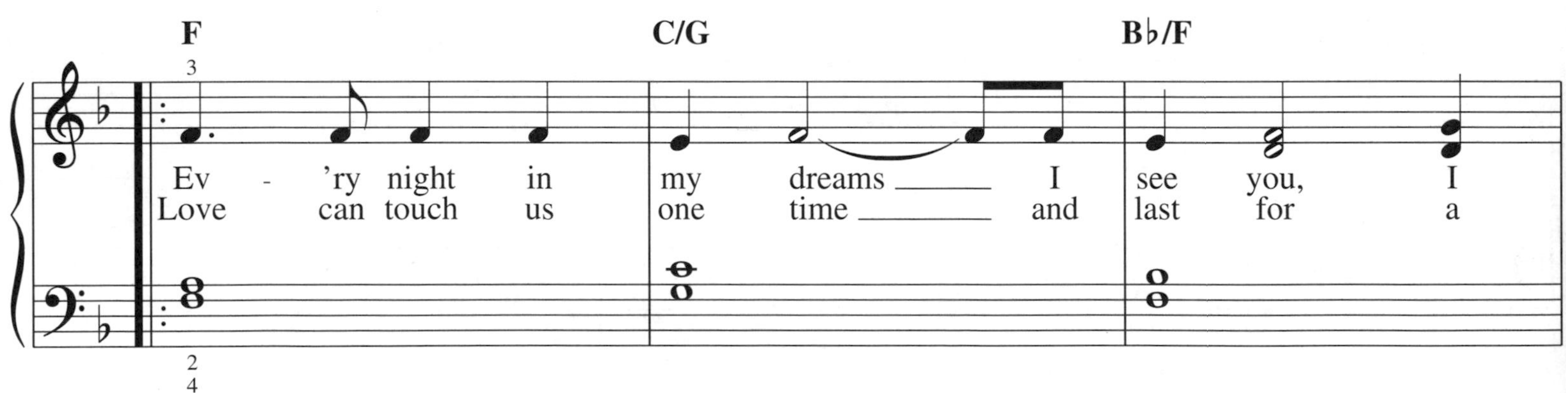

B♭
F
2
1
on.
gone.
Far a - cross the
Love was when I

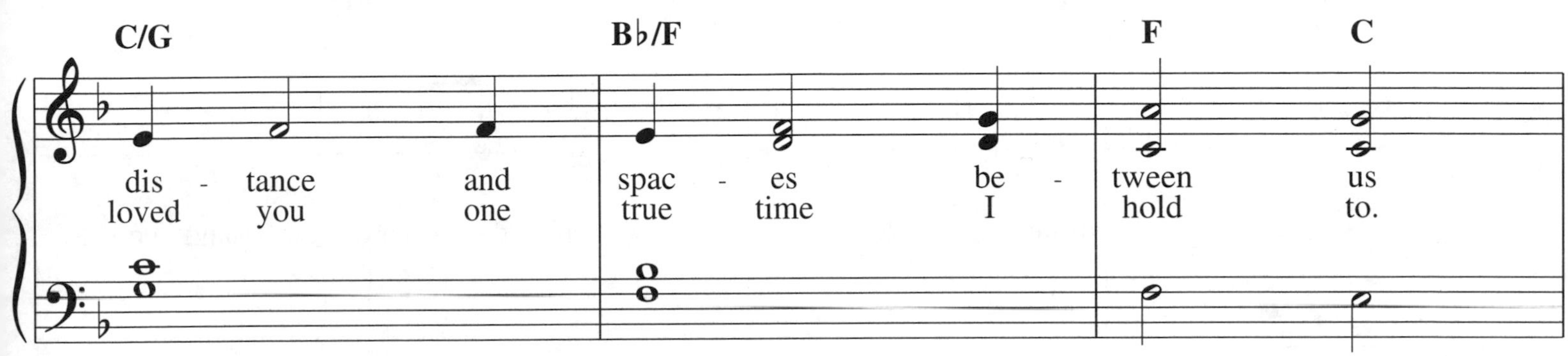
C/G
B♭/F
F
C
dis - tance and spac - es be - tween us
loved you one true time I hold to.

F
C/G
B♭
Am
1
you have come to show you go on.
In my life we'll al - ways go on.

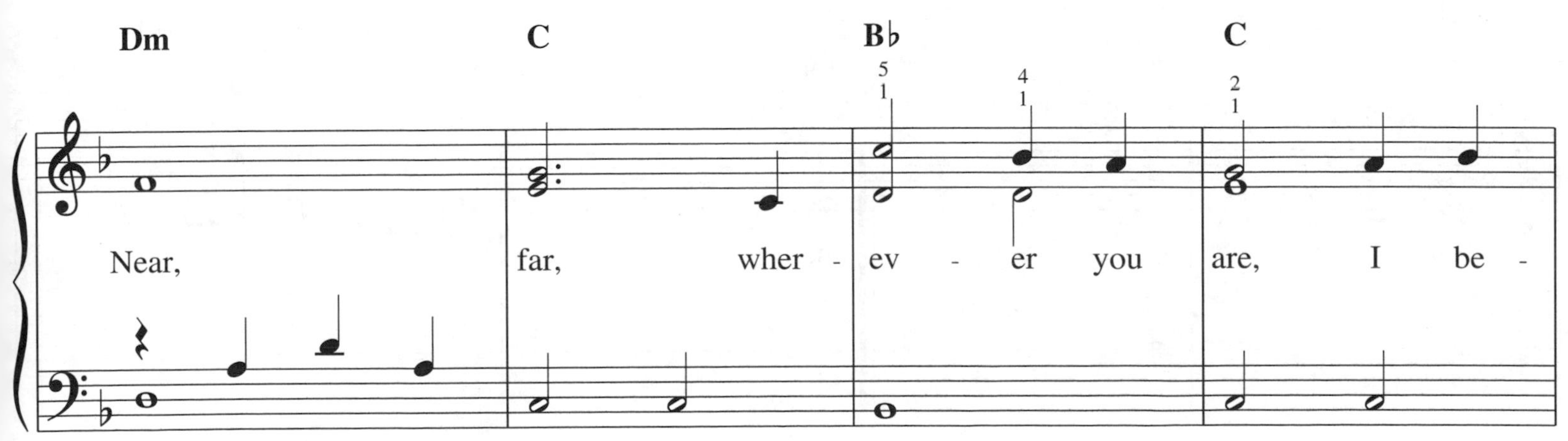
Dm
C
B♭
C
5
1
4
1
2
1
Near, far, wher - ev - er you are, I be -

Dm
C
B♭
Am
Gm
1
3
lieve that the heart does go on.

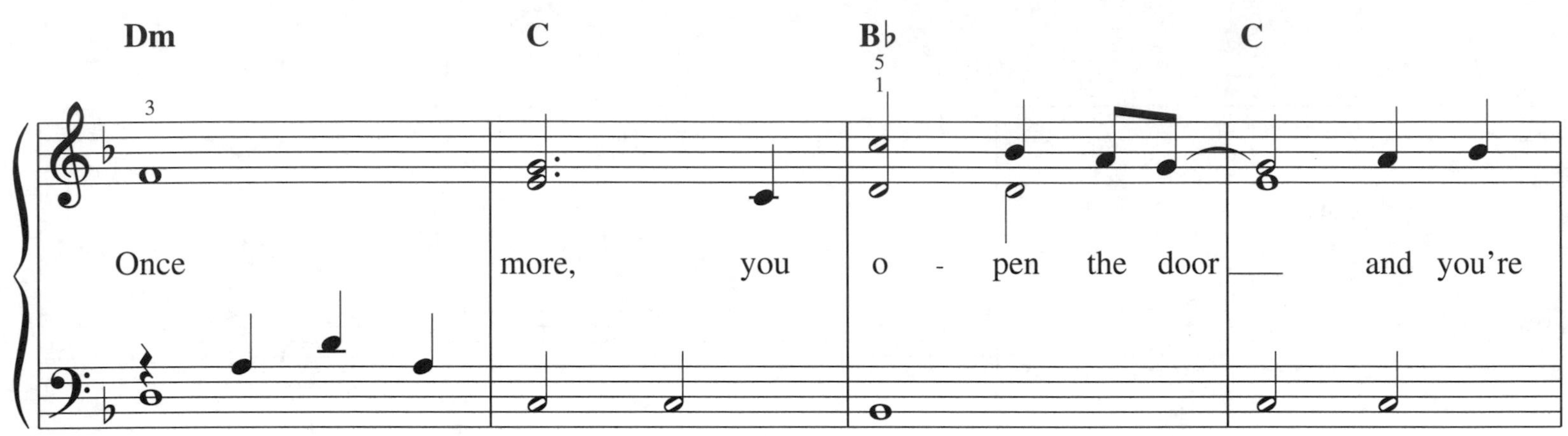
Dm
C
B♭
C
3
5
1
Once more, you o - pen the door and you're

Dm
C
B♭
2
here in my heart, and my heart will go

1.
2.
C
F
Dm
C
on and on.
on.

Slightly Slower

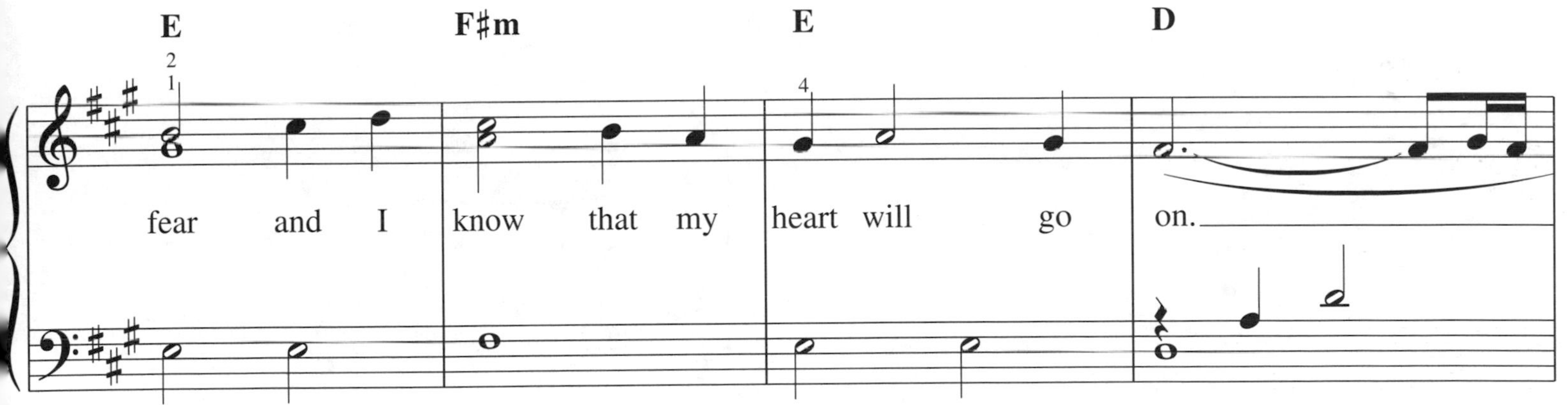

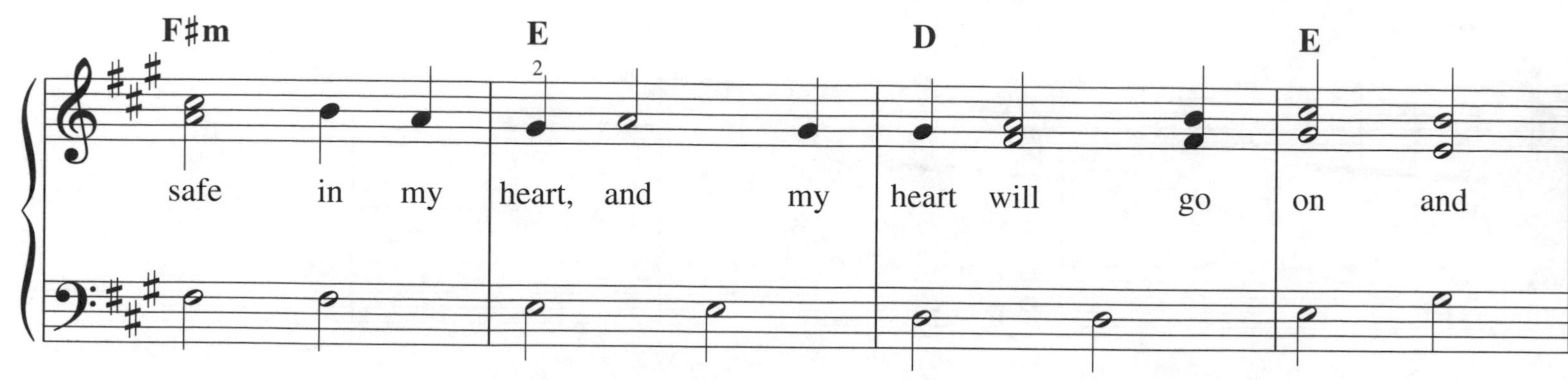
F♯m
E
D
E
2
safe in my heart, and my heart will go on and

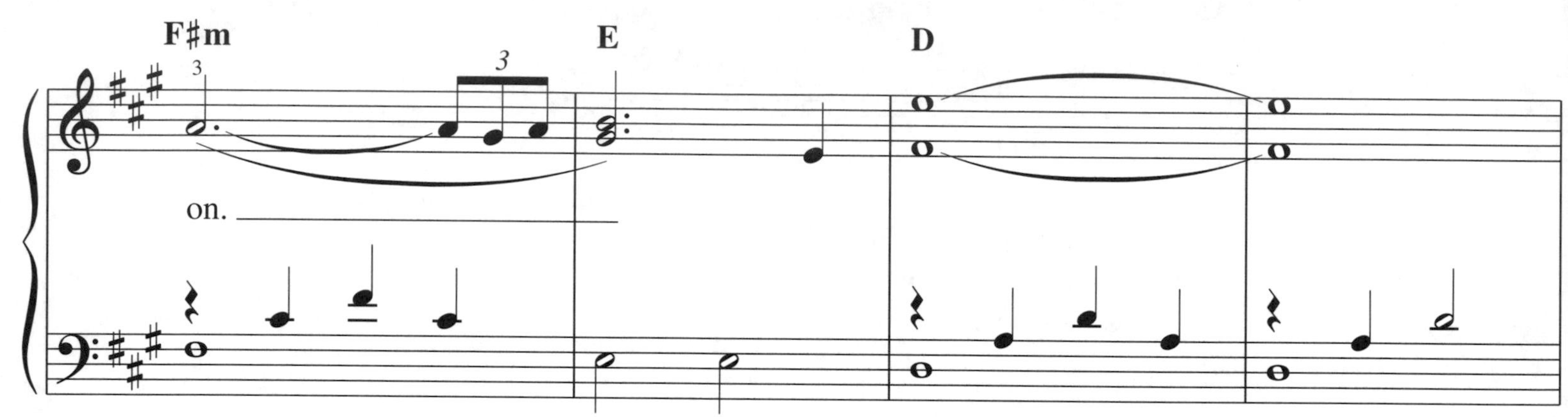
F♯m
E
D
3
3
on.

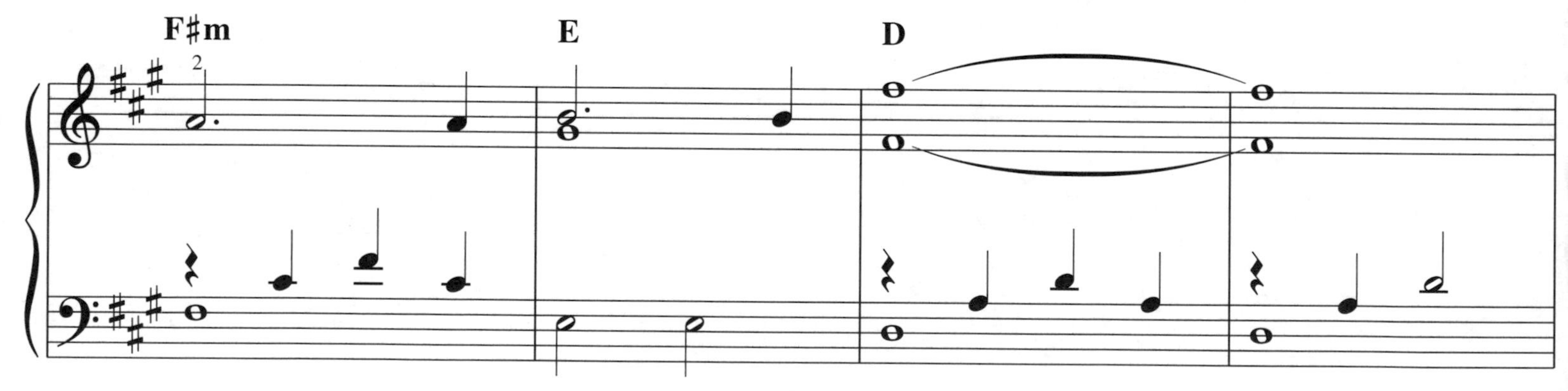
F♯m
E
D
2

F♯m
E
D

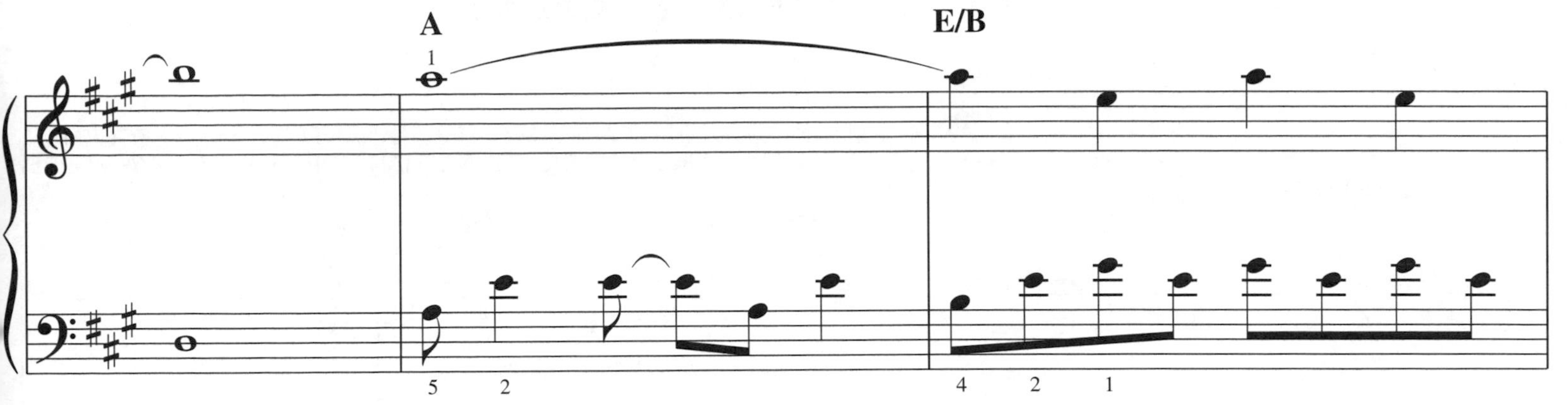
A
E/B
1
5 2
4 2 1

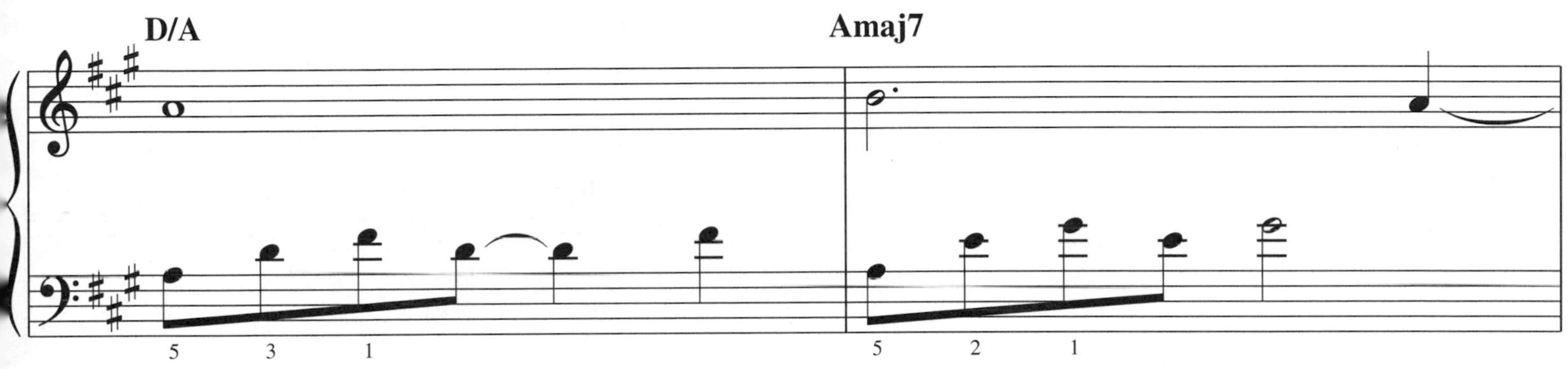
D/A
Amaj7
5 3 1
5 2 1

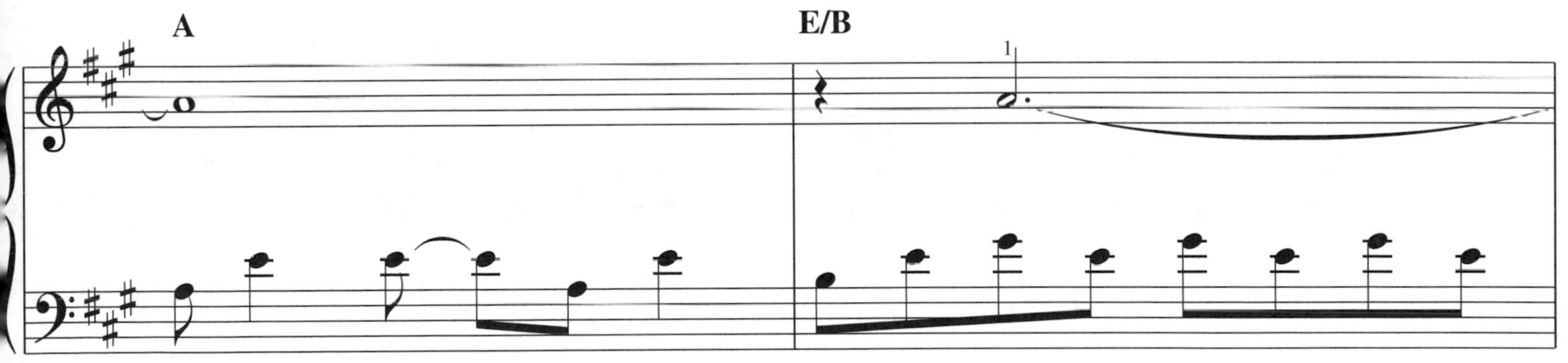
A
E/B
1

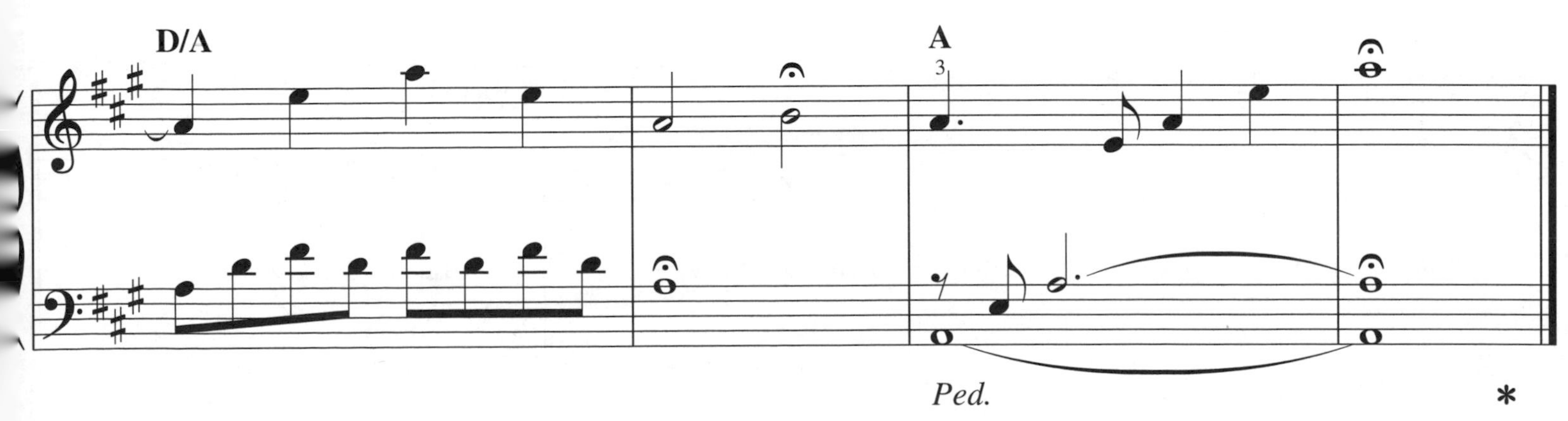
D/A
A
3
Ped.
*

ONE SWEET DAY

Words and Music by MARIAH CAREY, WALTER AFANASIEFF, SHAWN STOCKMAN, MICHAEL McCARY, NATHAN MORRIS and WANYA MORRIS

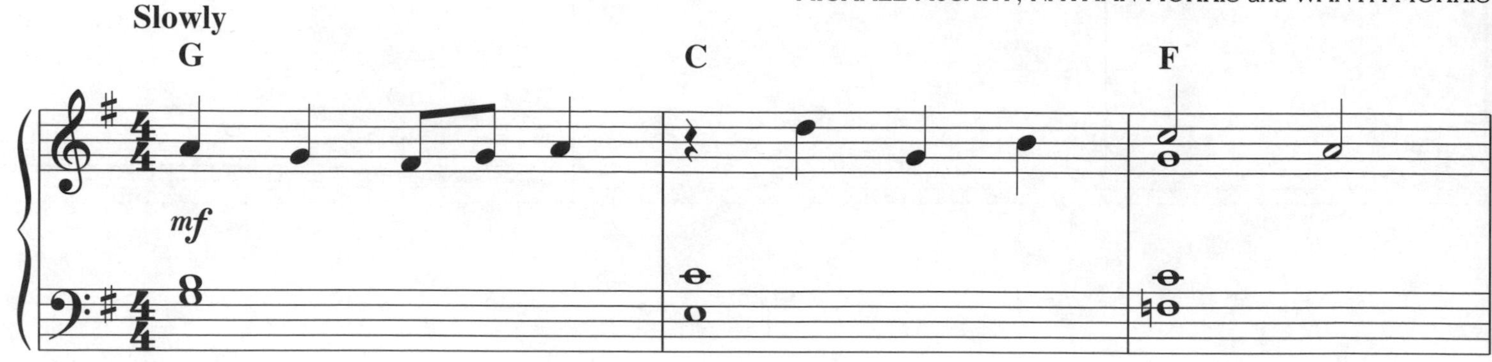

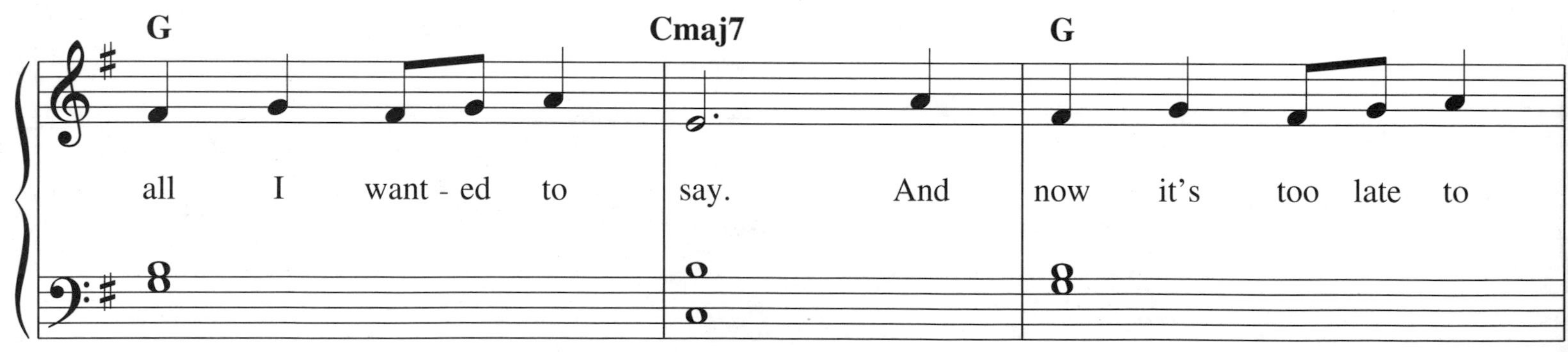

G
Cmaj7
G
Nev - er had I i - mag - ined liv - ing ___ with-out your
Dar - ling, I nev - er showed you, as - sumed you'd al - ways be

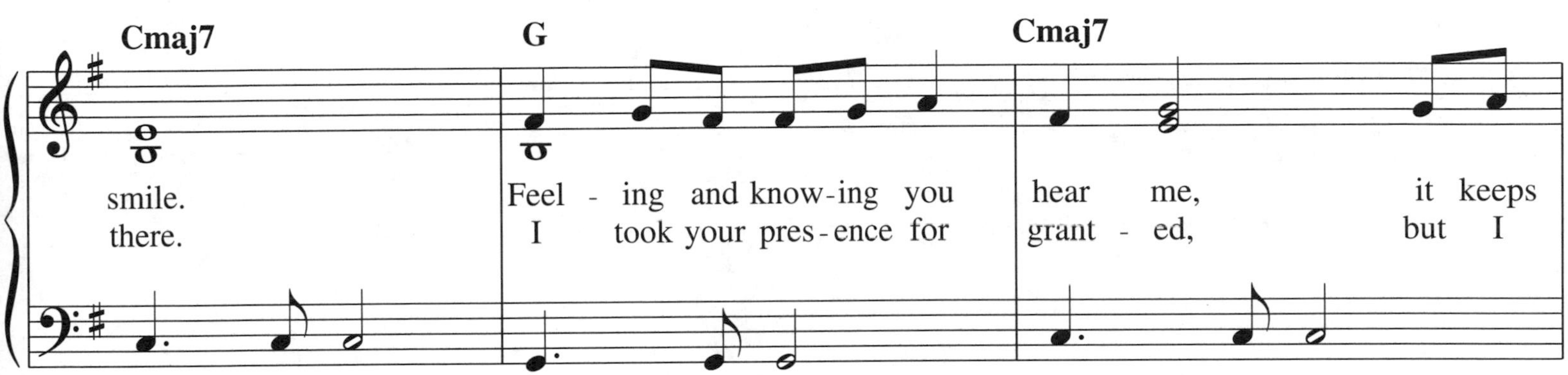
Cmaj7
G
Cmaj7
smile. Feel - ing and know-ing you hear me, it keeps
there. I took your pres - ence for grant - ed, but I

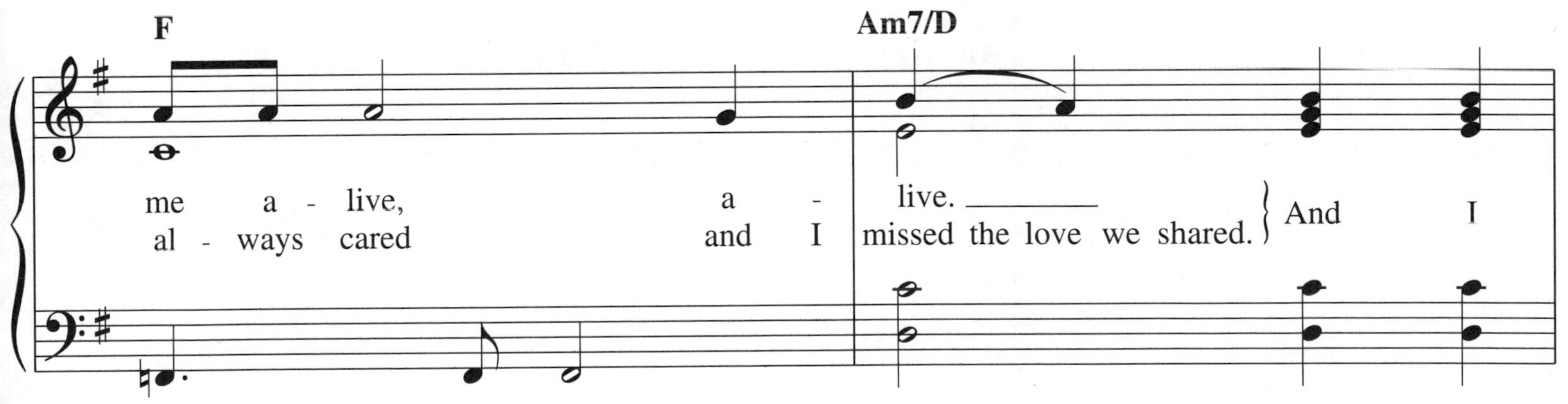
F
Am7/D
me a - live, a - live. ___
al - ways cared and I missed the love we shared.
And I

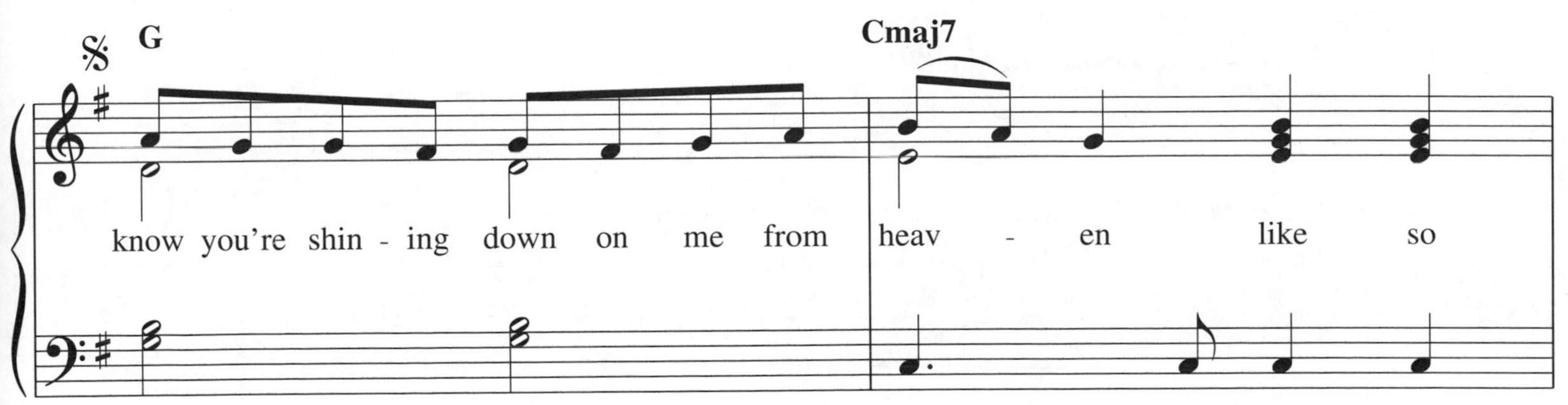
G
Cmaj7
know you're shin - ing down on me from heav - en like so

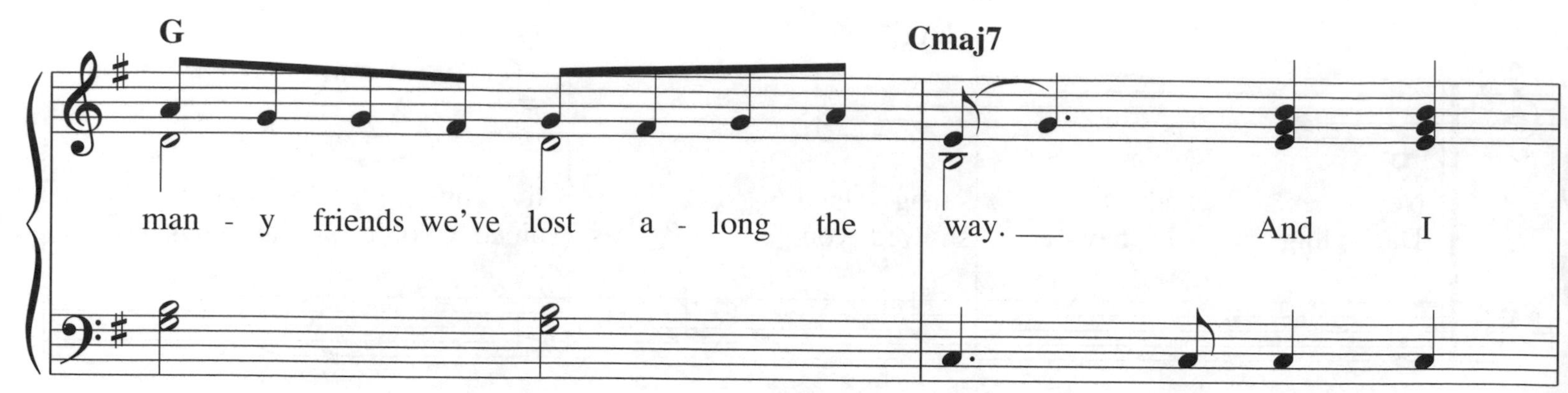
G
Cmaj7
man - y friends we've lost a - long the way. And I

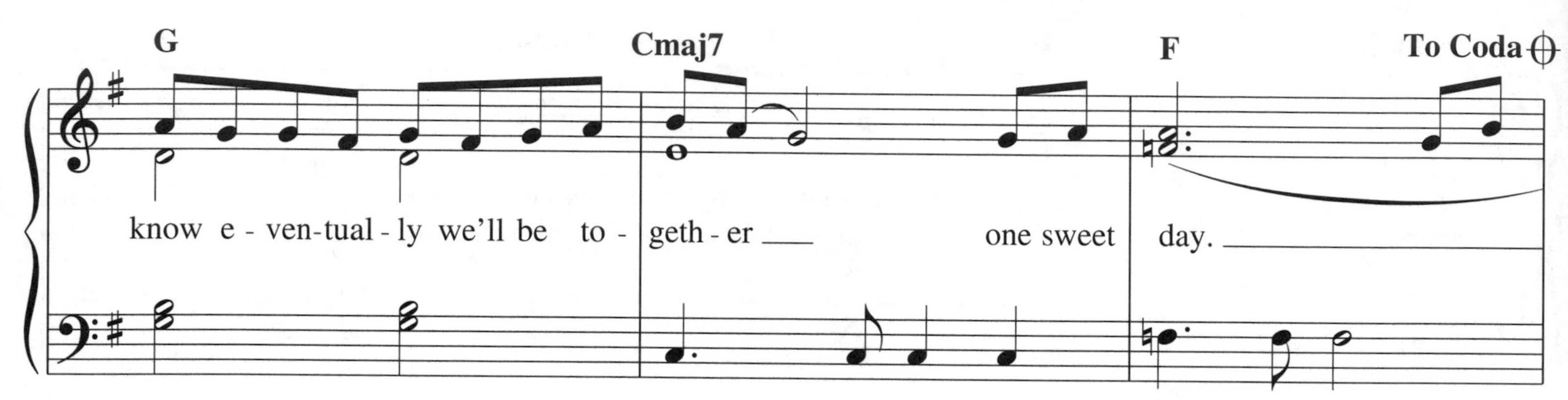
G
Cmaj7
F
To Coda
know e - ven-tual - ly we'll be to - geth - er one sweet day.

1.
2.
Am7/D
Am7/D
B7sus
B7
Al - though the

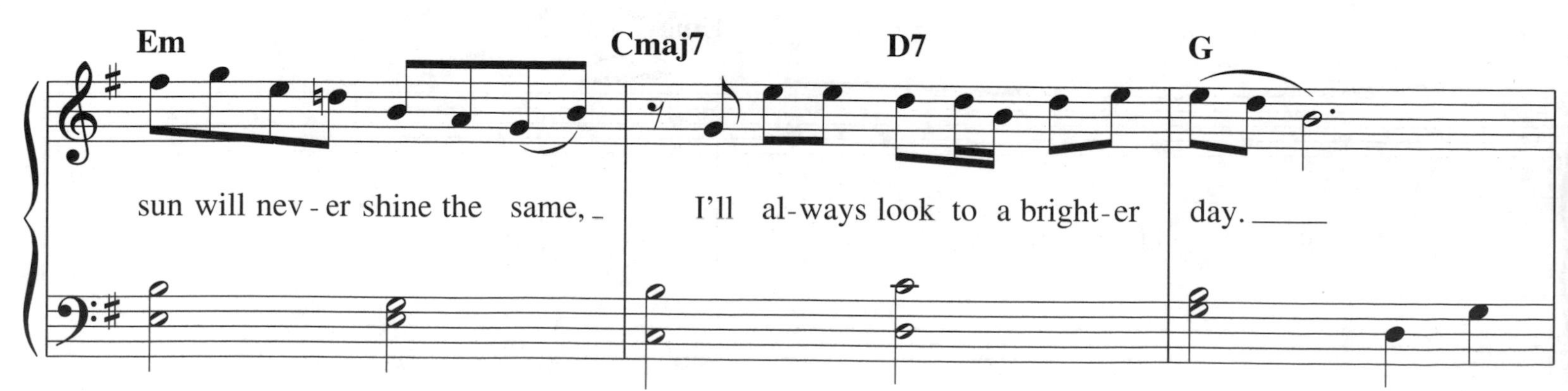
Em
Cmaj7
D7
G
sun will nev - er shine the same, I'll al-ways look to a bright-er day.

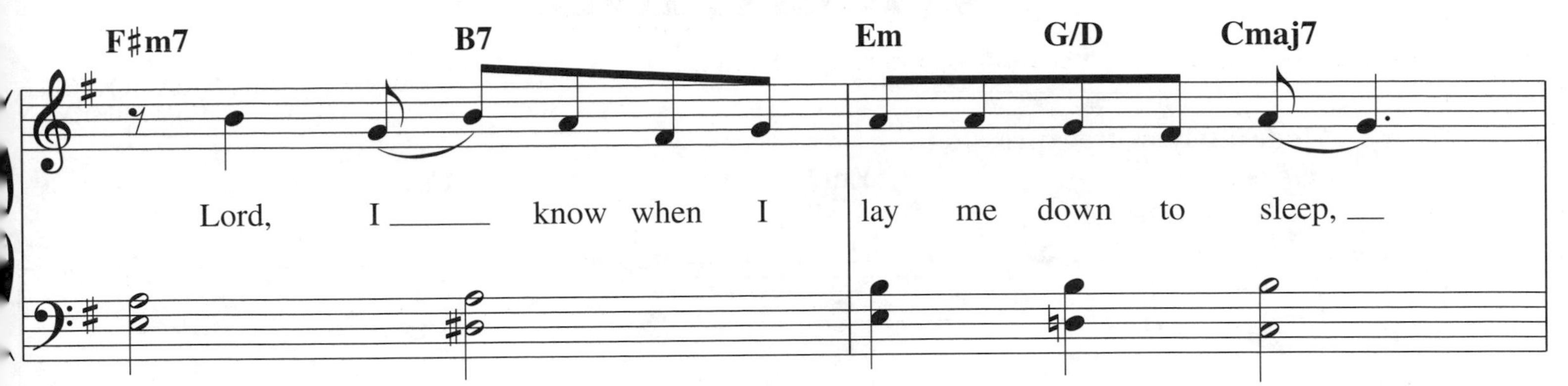
F♯m7
B7
Em
G/D
Cmaj7
Lord, I know when I lay me down to sleep,

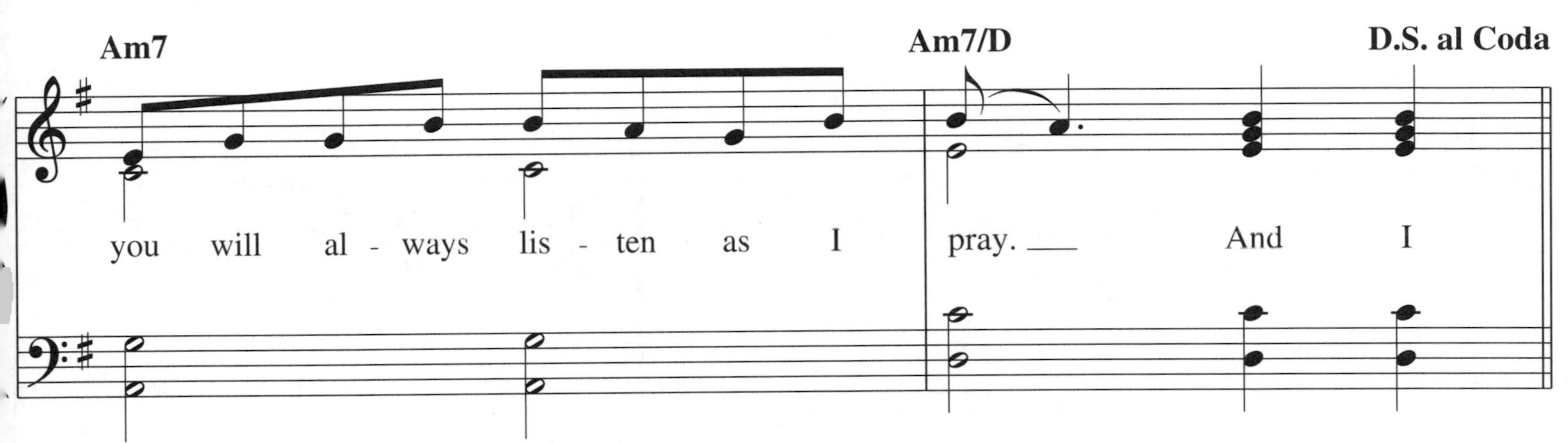
Am7
Am7/D
D.S. al Coda
you will al - ways lis - ten as I pray. And I

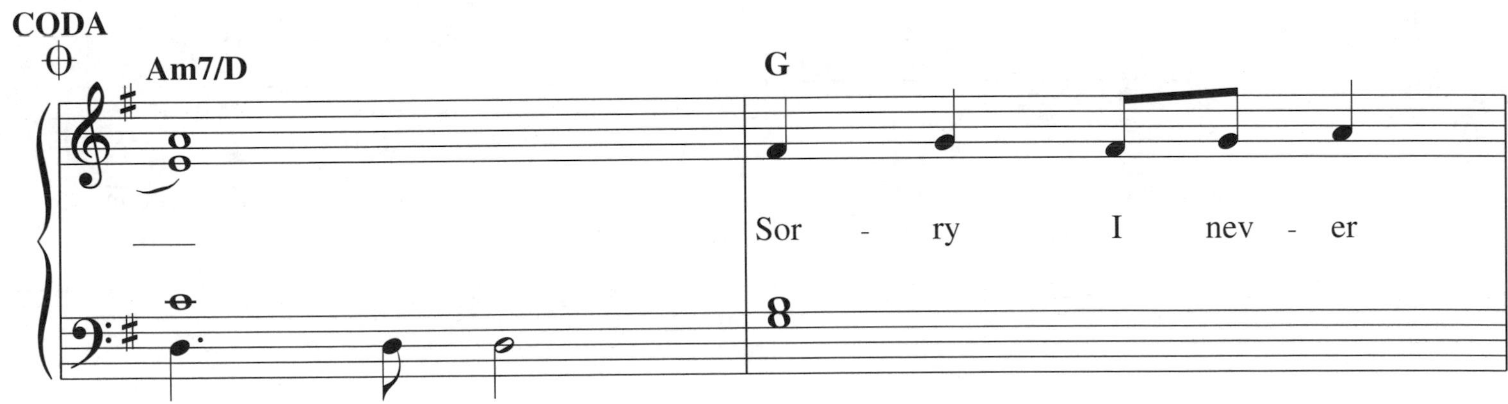
CODA
Am7/D
G
Sor - ry I nev - er

Cmaj7
G
Cmaj7
told you all I want - ed to say.

VALENTINE

Words and Music by JACK KUGELL
and JIM BRICKMAN

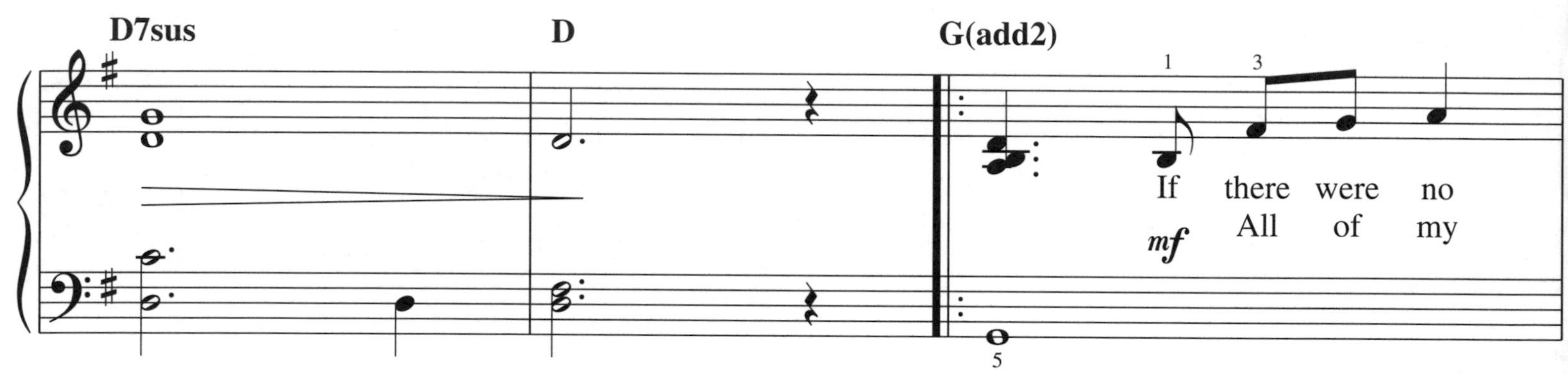

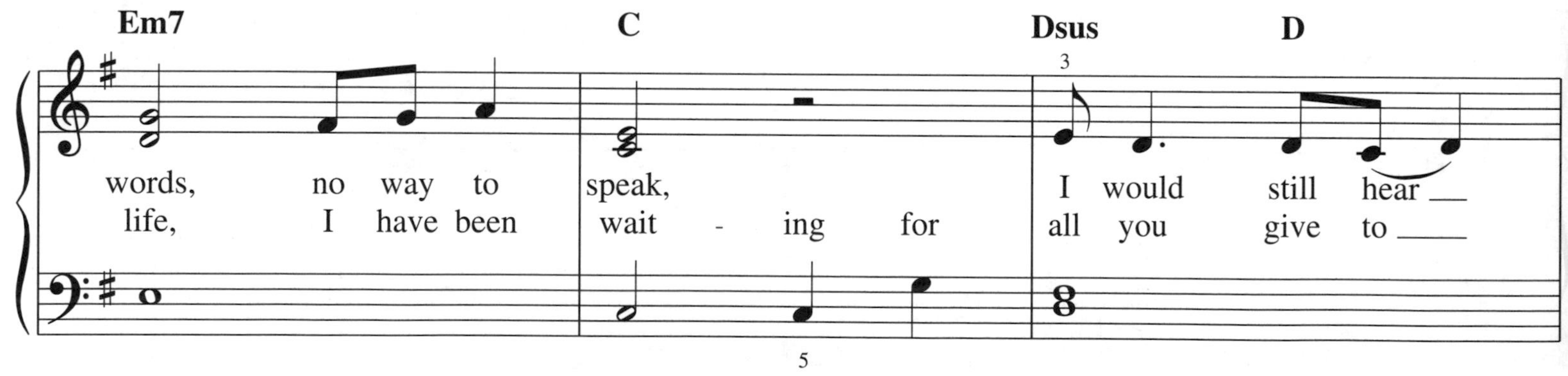

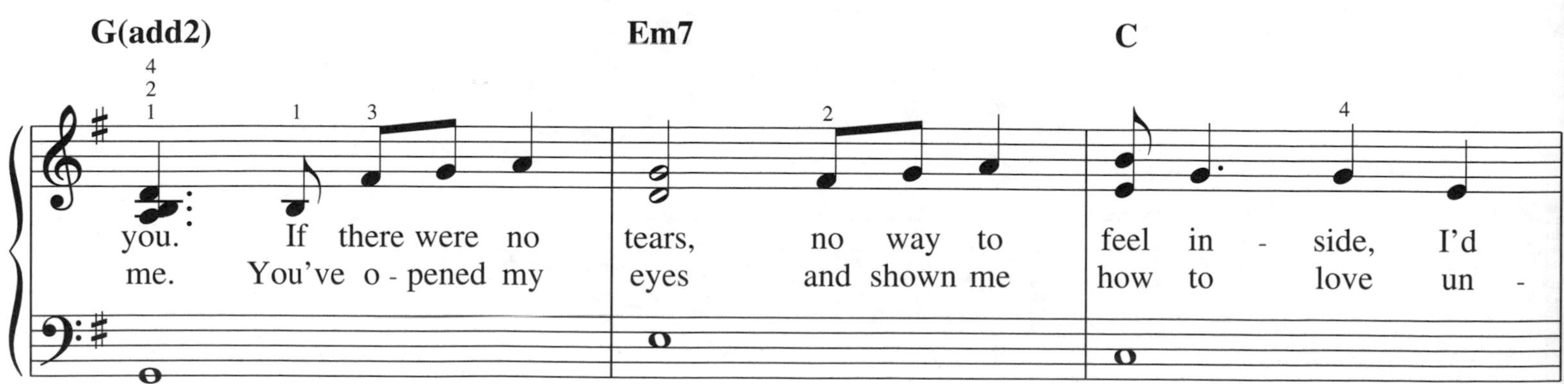

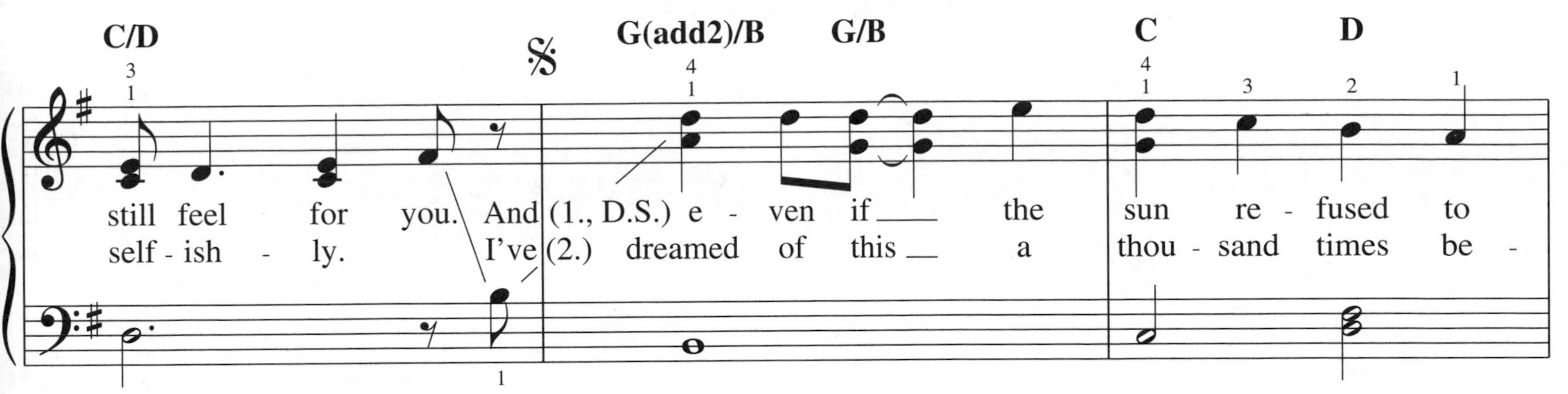
C/D
G(add2)/B
G/B
C
D
still feel for you. And (1., D.S.) e - ven if the sun re - fused to
self - ish - ly. I've (2.) dreamed of this a thou - sand times be -

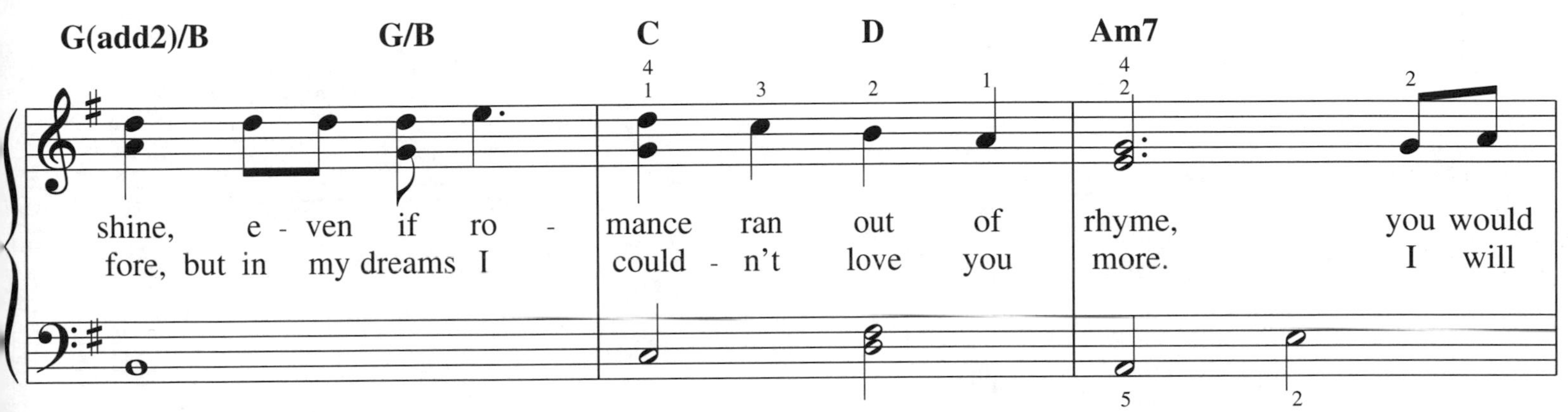
G(add2)/B
G/B
C
D
Am7
shine, e - ven if ro - mance ran out of rhyme, you would
fore, but in my dreams I could - n't love you more. I will

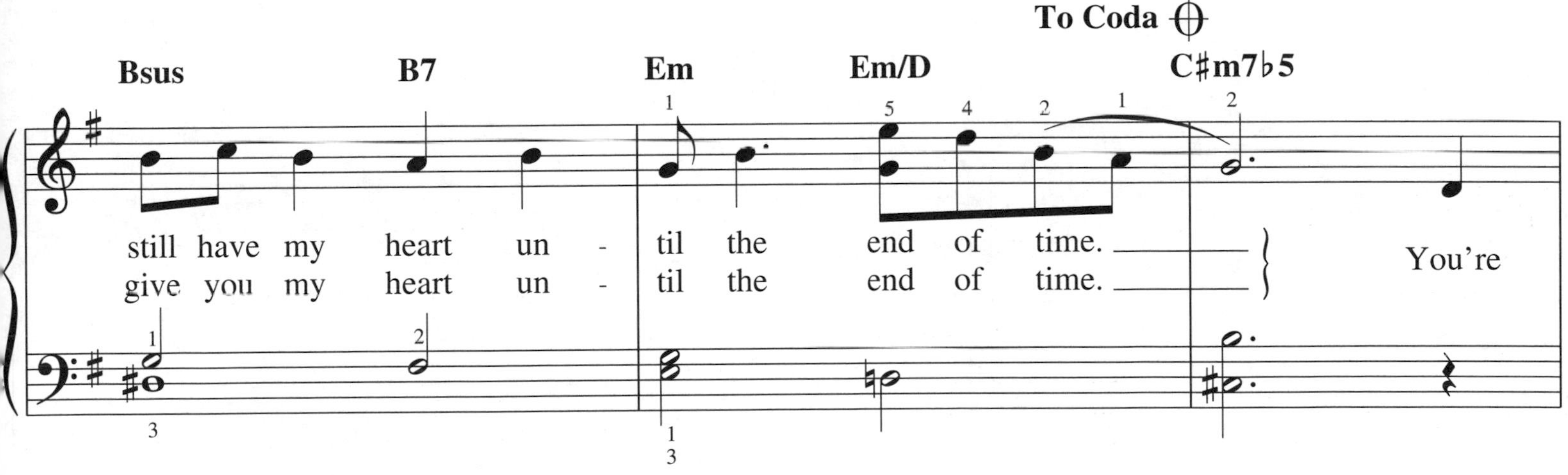
To Coda
Bsus
B7
Em
Em/D
C♯m7♭5
still have my heart un - til the end of time.
give you my heart un - til the end of time.
You're

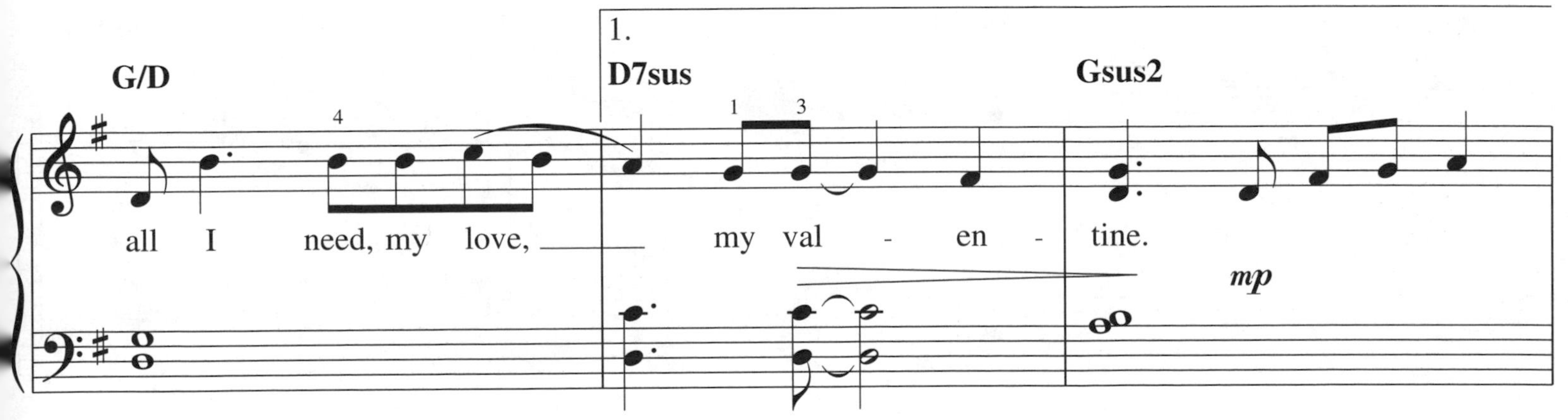
1.
G/D
D7sus
Gsus2
all I need, my love, my val - en - tine.
mp

Em7
Csus2
D7sus
D
2.
D7sus
G(add9)
Em7
my val - en - tine.
p
Csus2
C/E
D/F#
G
La, la, la, la, la,
la.
mp
p
Em7
C(add9)
Dsus
D.S. al Coda
And
mf

CODA
C♯m7♭5
G/D
D7sus
D7
'Cause all I need is you, my val - en -

Am7
G/B
Cmaj7
G/D
tine. Oh, oh. You're all I need, my love,

D7sus
Gsus2
Em7
my val - en - tine. Oh,
molto rit.
a tempo

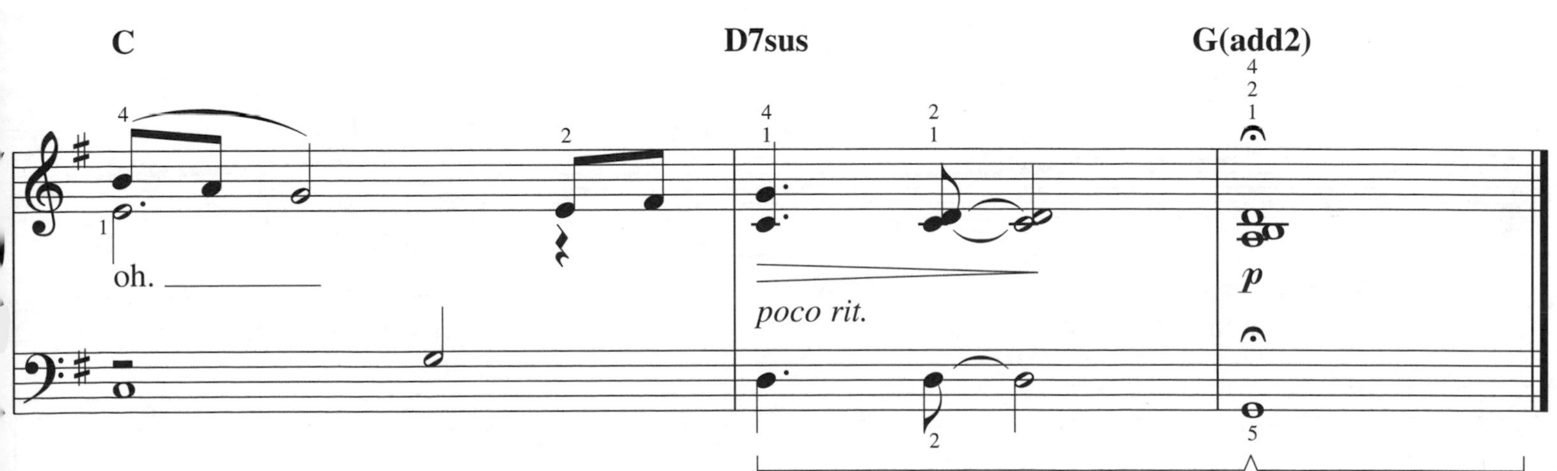
C
D7sus
G(add2)
oh.
poco rit.
p

WHEN YOU SAY NOTHING AT ALL

Words and Music by DON SCHLITZ
and PAUL OVERSTREET

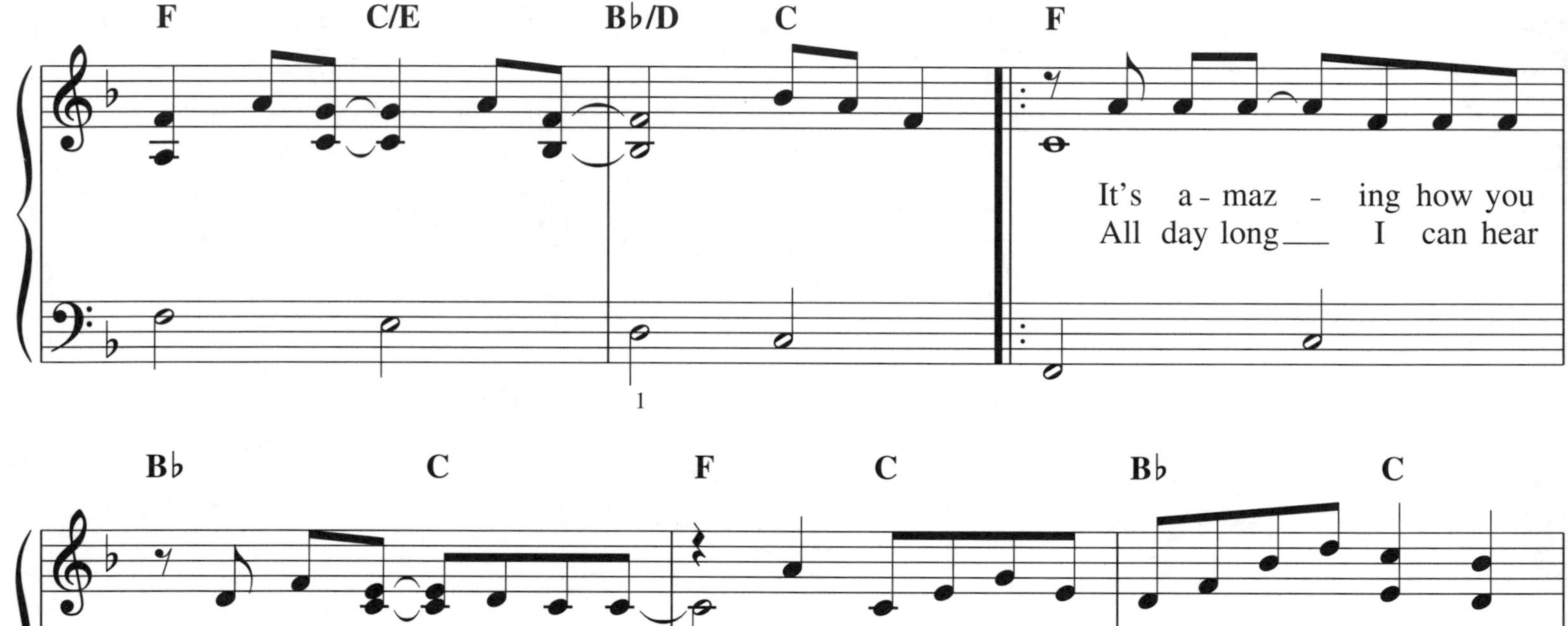

F
C
B♭
C
B♭
Try as I may I could nev -
Old Mis - ter Web - ster could nev -
C
F
B♭
- er ex - plain
- er de - fine
what I hear when you don't say a thing.
what's be - ing said be - tween your heart and mine.
C
F
C
The smile on your face lets me know
B♭
C
F
C
that you need me. There's a truth in your eyes say - ing you'll

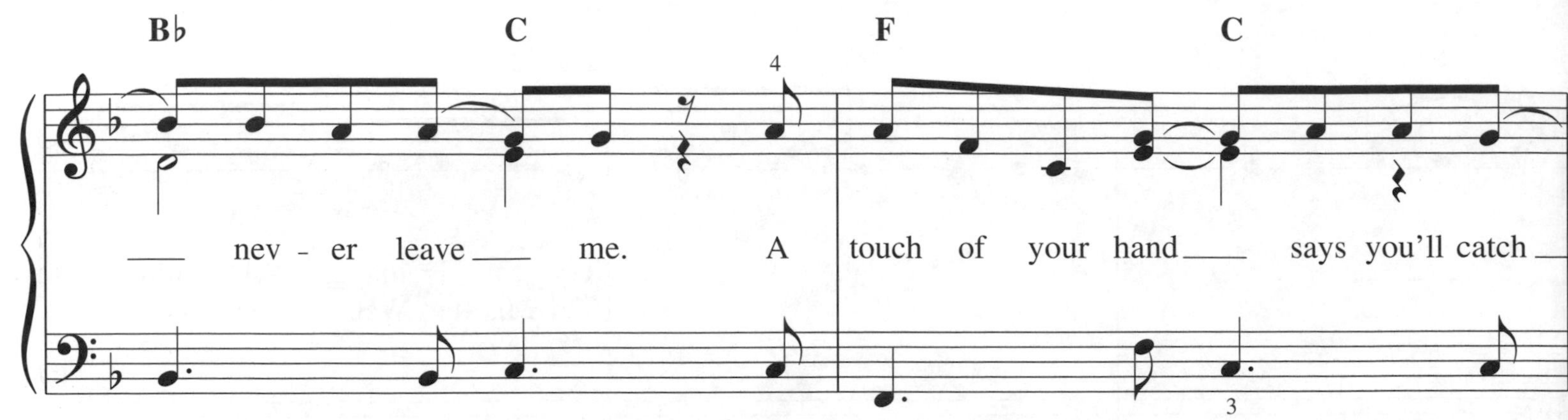
B♭
C
F
C
4
3
never leave me. A touch of your hand says you'll catch

B♭
C
B♭/D
C/E
F/A
5
4
me if ev - er I fall. Now

B♭
To Coda
1.
C
F
C
2
you say it best when you say noth-ing at all.

B♭
C
F
C/E
B/D
C
1

2.
C
F
C
3
1
when you say noth - ing at all.

D.S. al Coda
B♭
C
F
C
B♭
3
The

CODA
C
3
1
F
C
B♭
C
when you say noth-ing at all.

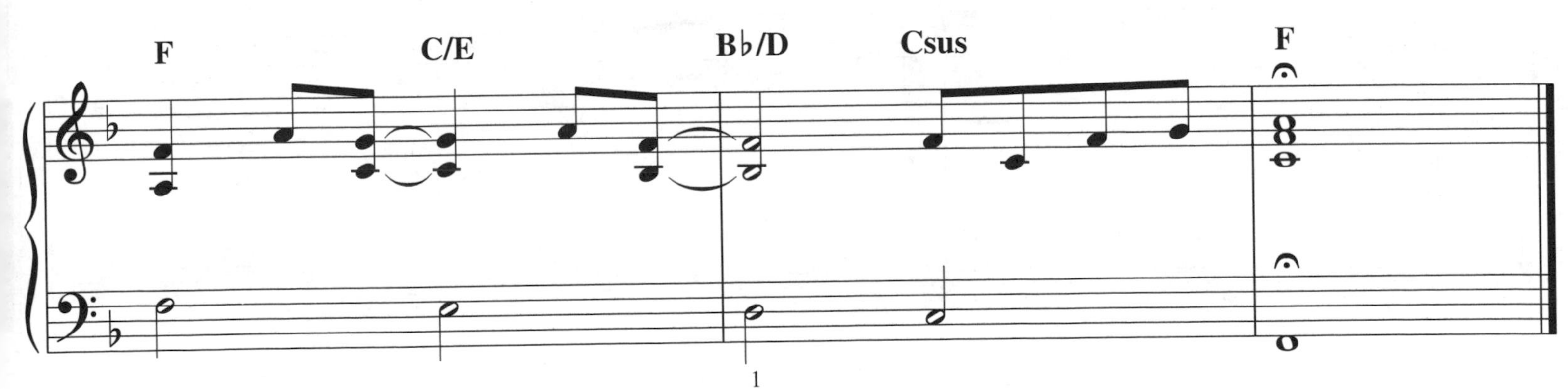
F
C/E
B♭/D
Csus
F
1

SOMETHING ABOUT THE WAY YOU LOOK TONIGHT

Words and Music by ELTON JOHN
and BERNIE TAUPIN

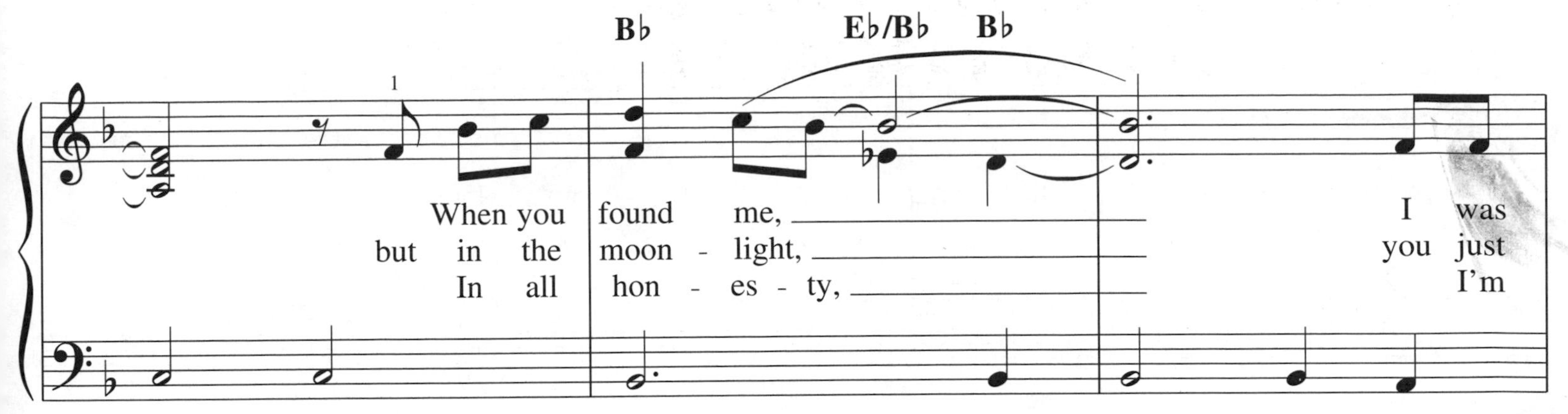
B♭
E♭/B♭
B♭
When you found me, I was
but in the moon - light, you just
In all hon - es - ty, I'm

Gm7
C
F/C
C
feel - ing like a cloud a - cross the sun.
shine like a bea - con of the bay.
speech - less and I don't know where to start.

1.
2.,3.
F/C
C
Well, I need to

F
And I can't ex - plain, but there's

A7
Dm
some-thing a - bout the way you look to - night,

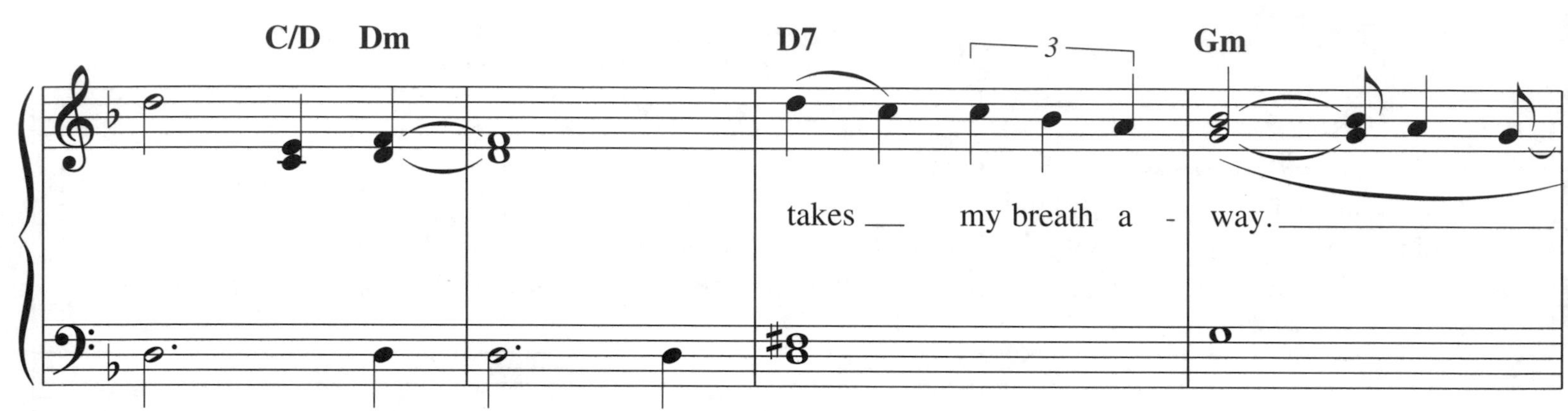
C/D Dm
D7
Gm
3
takes my breath a - way.

Gm7
It's that feel - ing I get a - bout you

C F/C C
F/C C
2
deep in - side.
And I can't de -

F
A7
scribe,
but there's some-thing a - bout the way

Dm
Dm7/C
B♭
you look to - night,

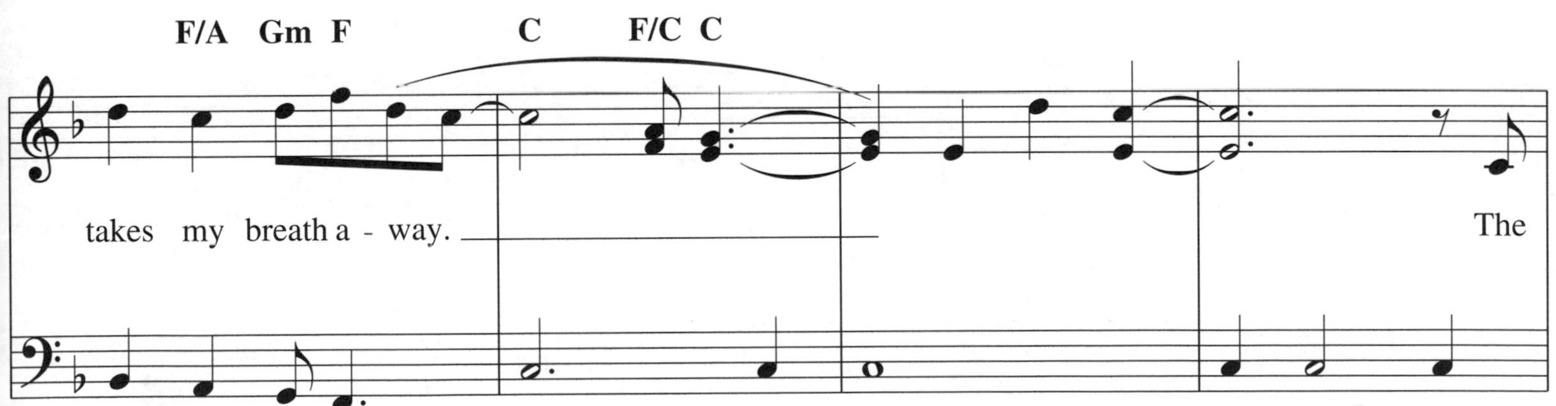
F/A Gm F
C
F/C C
takes my breath a - way.
The

C7
To Coda
F
N.C.
F
way you look to - night.

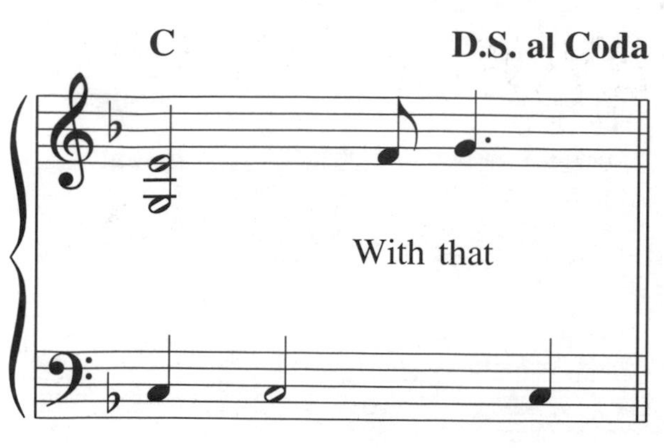
C
D.S. al Coda
With that

CODA
F
B♭/F
F
night,

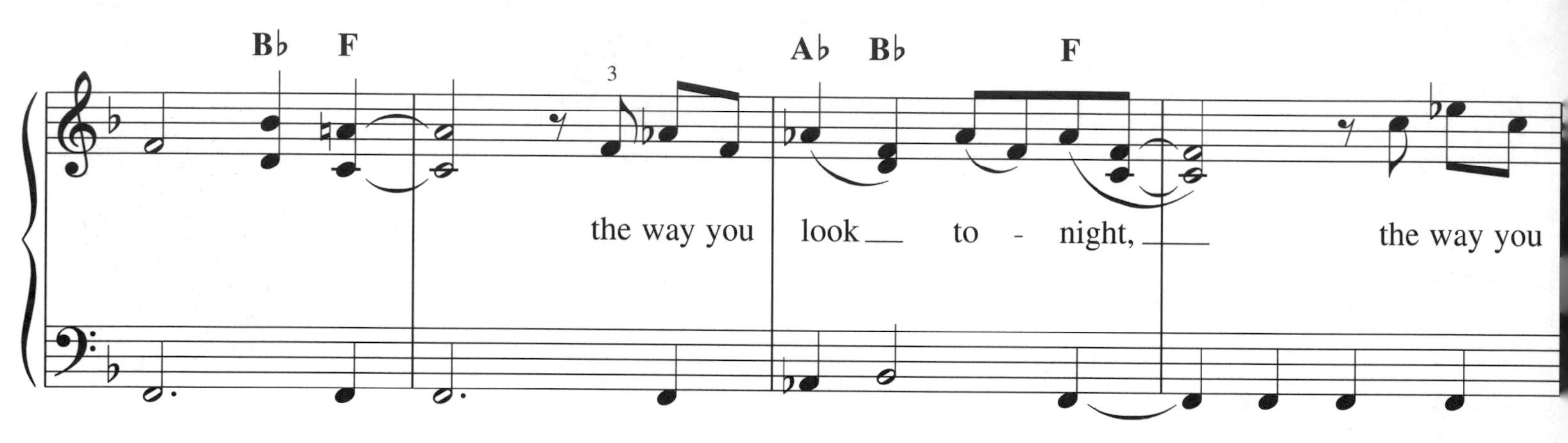
B♭
F
A♭
B♭
F
the way you
look to - night,
the way you

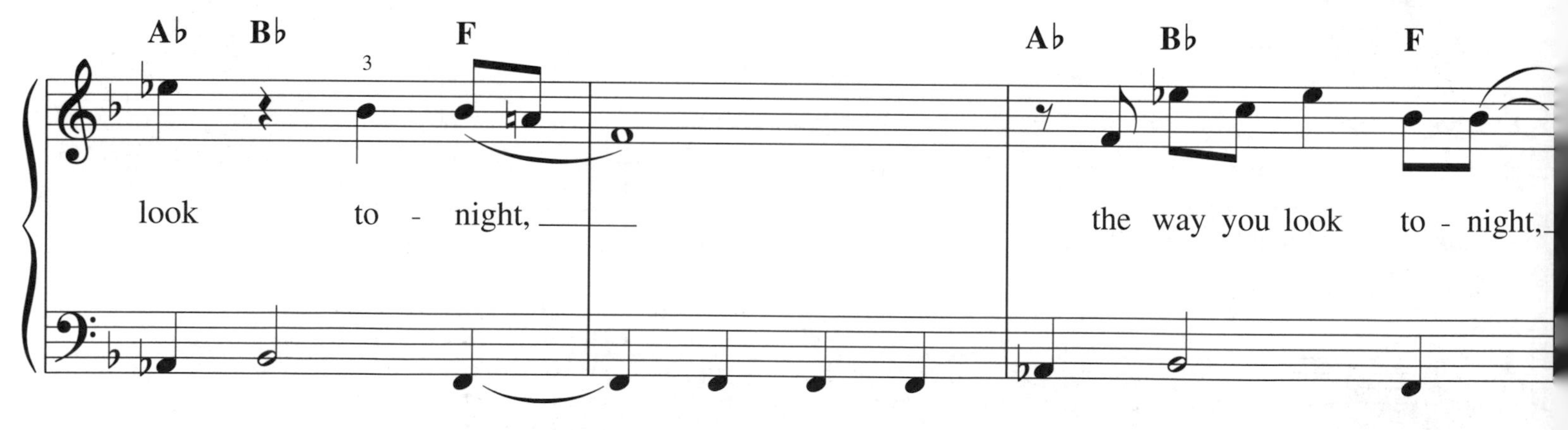
A♭
B♭
F
A♭
B♭
F
look to - night,
the way you look to - night,

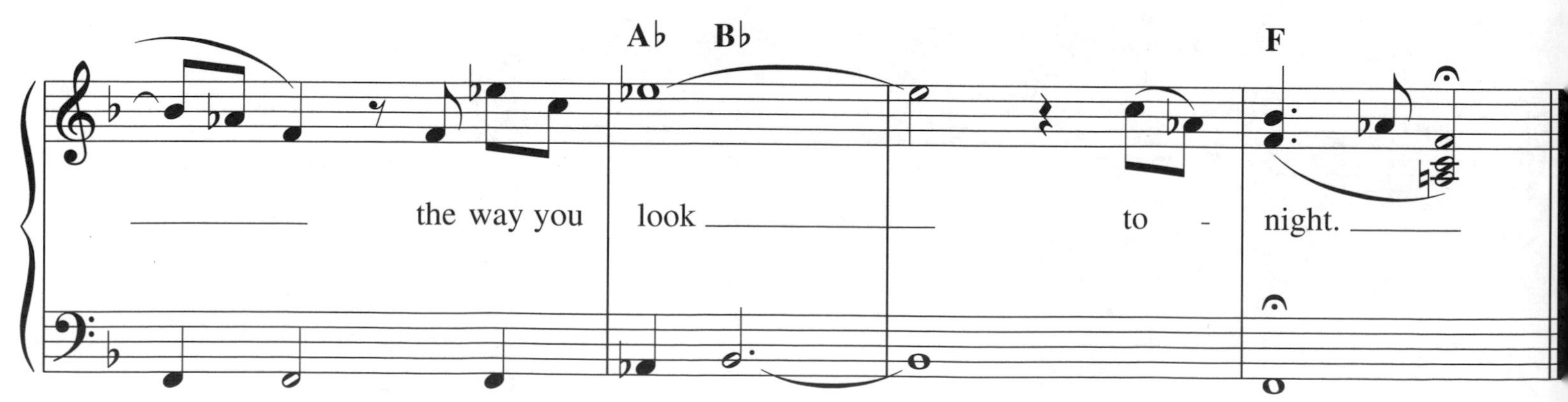
A♭
B♭
F
the way you
look
to - night.

It's Easy To Play Your Favorite Songs with Hal Leonard Easy Piano Books

The Best of Today's Movie Hits
16 contemporary film favorites: Change The World • Colors Of The Wind • I Believe In You And Me • I Finally Found Someone • If I Had Words • Mission: Impossible Theme • When I Fall In Love • You Must Love Me • more.
00310248...$9.95

Playing The Blues
Over 30 great blues tunes arranged for easy piano: Baby, Won't You Please Come Home • Chicago Blues • Fine And Mellow • Heartbreak Hotel • Pinetop's Blues • St. Louis Blues • The Thrill Is Gone • more.
00310102...$12.95

The Best Songs Ever - 3rd Edition
A prestigious collection of 80 all-time favorite songs, featuring: All I Ask Of You • Beauty and the Beast • Body And Soul • Candle In The Wind • Crazy • Don't Know Much • Endless Love • Fly Me To The Moon • The Girl From Ipanema • Here's That Rainy Day • Imagine • In The Mood • Let It Be • Longer • Moonlight In Vermont • People • Satin Doll • Save The Best For Last • Somewhere Out There • Stormy Weather • Strangers In The Night • Tears In Heaven • What A Wonderful World • When I Fall In Love • and more
00359223 ....$19.95

Country Love Songs
34 classic and contemporary country favorites, including: The Dance • A Few Good Things Remain • Forever And Ever Amen • I Never Knew Love • Love Can Build A Bridge • Love Without End, Amen • She Believes In Me • She Is His Only Need • Where've You Been • and more.
00110030...$12.95

R&B Love songs
27 songs, including: Ain't Nothing Like The Real Thing • Easy • Exhale (Shoop Shoop) • The First Time Ever I Saw Your Face • Here And Now • I'm Your Baby Tonight • My Girl • Never Can Say Goodbye • Ooo Baby Baby • Save The Best For Last • Someday • Still • and more.
00310181 ....$12.95

Rock N Roll For Easy Piano
40 rock favorites for the piano, including: All Shook Up • At The Hop • Chantilly Lace • Great Balls Of Fire • Lady Madonna • The Shoop Shoop Song (It's In His Kiss) • The Twist • Wooly Bully • and more.
00222544...$12.95

I'll Be Seeing You
50 Songs Of World War II
A salute to the music and memories of WWII, including a chronology of events on the homefront, dozens of photos, and 50 radio favorites of the GIs and their families back home. Includes: Boogie Woogie Bugle Boy • Don't Sit Under The Apple Tree (With Anyone Else But Me) • I Don't Want To Walk Without You • Moonlight In Vermont • and more.
00310147...$17.95

Disney's The Hunchback Of Notre Dame Selections
10 selections from Disney's animated classic, complete with beautiful color illustrations. Includes: The Bells Of Notre Dame • God Help The Outcasts • Out There • Someday • and more.
00316011...$14.95

Today's Love Songs
31 contemporary favorites, including: All I Ask Of You • Because I Love You • Don't Know Much • Endless Love • Forever And Ever, Amen • Here And Now • I'll Be Loving You Forever • Lost In Your Eyes • Love Without End, Amen • Rhythm Of My Heart • Unchained Melody • Vision Of Love • and more.
00222541...$14.95

Best Of Cole Porter
Over 30 songs, including: Be A Clown • Begin The Beguine • Easy To Love • From This Moment On • In The Still Of The Night • Night And Day • So In Love • Too Darn Hot • You Do Something To Me • You'd Be So Nice To Come Home To • and more
00311576...$14.95

For More Information, See Your Local Music Dealer, Or Write To:

7777 W. Bluemound Rd. P.O. Box 13819 Milwaukee, WI 53213

Prices, book contents, and availability subject to change without notice

0597